C000072517

THE
SHEFFIELD
WEDNESDAY
MISCELLANY

DARREN PHILLIPS

First published in 2011 by
The History Press
The Mill, Brimscombe Port
Stroud, Gloucestershire, GL5 2QG
www.thehistorypress.co.uk

British Library Cataloguing in Publication Data.
A catalogue record for this book is available from the British
Library.

ISBN 978 0 7524 5955 4

Typesetting and origination by The History Press
Printed in Great Britain

IN THE BEGINNING
THERE WAS CRICKET

On 4 September 1867 Sheffield Wednesday, or The Wednesday as they were known at the time, came into being. The venture was the brainchild of a small group of men who saw the establishment of an Association Football team as a perfect counterpart to the Wednesday Cricket Club.

Cricketers had been thudding leather against willow for the past 47 years but had eagerly watched a new sport grow in public appeal. There was little choice. Sheffield was the centre of European, if not world, soccer at the time, with a host of clubs established throughout the latter part of the nineteenth century. The city had hosted the first ever recognised football game when Sheffield played Hallam on 12 February 1861. Football fever may have been spreading across the world as the 1870s approached, but in South Yorkshire the bug had been at epidemic proportions for the best part of a decade.

There was also a realisation that further sporting endeavour would bind the team together for an entire calendar year thus reducing the chance of defections over the winter months when no cricket was played. It would also keep their players in good physical condition until the summer.

In the long term that footballing arm eclipsed the cricketing one, so much so that the soccer players broke away in 1883 becoming a wholly separate entity. As a point of note the Wednesday Cricket Club ceased to be in 1924; support and, as a consequence, finances had dwindled because of football's popularity. The split also meant those men who preferred leather on willow to inflated rubber bladders encased in heavy brown leather led a nomadic existence playing at various grounds.

Adding insult to no small amount of injury the footballers met their cricketing counterparts in 1911 scoring a 55-run win after bowling the summer men out for less than 100 runs.

One hundred years after that encounter Sheffield Wednesday fans set about rising a phoenix from the ashes and the Wednesday Cricket Club was re-formed. An XI competed in local league cricket – Division C of the Irwin Mitchell Alliance Midweek League – from the 2011 season with home games played at Abbeydale Park.

WHAT'S IN A NAME?

Why was Wednesday chosen as a name? Simply because the club's originators and players took afternoons off work on that day to realise their sporting ambitions. Maybe by coincidence or even design the gathering of the football club's founding fathers took place on a Wednesday at the Adelphi pub situated on the site now occupied by the Crucible Theatre – home of many artistic productions and the annual World Snooker Championships – at the junction of Arundel and Sycamore Street. The word Sheffield was only officially added to the club's title just ahead of the 1929/30 season when the Football Association sanctioned it, although this prospect had first been mooted two years earlier. Additionally when residency was taken up at the Olive Grove 32 years earlier a stand had 'Sheffield Wednesday' painted along the roof.

FIRST IMPRESSIONS

Wednesday played their first game against The Mechanics Club at Norfolk Park during October 1867 just weeks after coming into being. A comfortable 3–0 win was scored. In a fashion similar to the sport of Aussie Rules Football, Wednesday also hit four unanswered 'rouges'. This was a system of scoring then known as Sheffield Rules. Flag posts were erected alongside the more recognisable goalposts and a rouge would be scored when the ball was put through this outer sector and subsequently touched down. If scores were level then rouges would provide a tie-breaker.

A village team from Dronfield were next up on 31 December 1867. A field in Sam Baggaley's farm was the venue. Wednesday persevered winning 1–0 hitting four rouges while conceding none.

HOME TURF

Sheffield Wednesday's name is inextricably linked with Hillsborough but the club spent many of its formative years playing at various grounds dotted around the city. Bramall Lane was an ad hoc venue until 1888 but the club's first home – occupied between 1867 and 1869 – was Highfield. Myrtle Road was used for just under a decade with Sheaf House the club's next home. That tenure lasted a full 10 years until paying a chunk of ever-increasing gate money to landlords irked The Wednesday board who set about finding a new home. They chose the Olive Grove, a small site adjacent to the Midland Railway near Queen's Road, leased from the Duke of Norfolk, on which an olive farm once existed. At the club's own expense the area was enclosed.

The Olive Grove staged its first match on 12 September 1887 – a friendly against Blackburn Rovers. Wednesday's Billy Mosforth was the first player to find the net there although honours finished even at 4–4, despite the visitors holding a three-goal lead at one point. The club continued to call the Grove home for 12 years even though it boasted very little in the way of creature comforts. There were no dressing rooms for some time, forcing the players to change in the Earl of

Arundel pub and Surrey Hotel. Had it not been for the owners seeking to develop the land for track expansion, Wednesday may have stayed for a few years longer than they did.

Although given time to vacate, Wednesday could see no point staying where they were not wanted so found new land quite quickly. The site currently occupied was originally named Owlerton Stadium and bought for £5,000 after sufficient funds were raised through a share issue. There was a possibility of a site being utilised in Carbrook. This option was popular, as making Owlerton home meant a move across the city to an area surrounded by green fields. However, Carbrook was eventually rejected and Owlerton adopted.

Residency was taken up during late 1899 and in 1914 the stadium was renamed Hillsborough. The first league season after the move saw Wednesday go an entire campaign without dropping a single home point. The only blemish on the record was a reverse in the FA Cup – to Sheffield United. Chesterfield were the first visitors to Owlerton where 12,000 spectators saw Wednesday coast to a 5–1 win despite falling behind – an act which meant Herbert Munday had the honour of scoring the first goal. A symbolic kick-off was performed by the then Lord Mayor of Sheffield, and former Wednesday player, Councillor William Clegg.

RELICS OF THE SOUTH STAND

A remarkable aspect of the present-day Hillsborough is that many of its original features remain. These include the South Stand, originally a brick-by-brick replica of the Olive Grove's main stand. Designed by Archibald Leitch at a cost of £18,000 it was first pressed into service in January 1914 for an FA Cup tie with Notts County, the Owls running out 3–2 winners. The stand became all-seater in 1965 with a roof added during 1992 necessitating a 125-metre steel girder, thought to be the longest single structure of its type in Britain. Despite development for the Euro '96 tournament and the addition of another tier, these renovations were made on the original structure from 1899. Other original features of the stand still in use include the clock – which came from the Olive Grove – and the finial which surrounds it.

GROUNDING DOWN THE COSTS

Wednesday's board has never been afraid to innovate and, when erected, the North Stand boasted the country's second cantilevered roof – although it was actually the only one to run uninterrupted along the full length of a football pitch. The £150,000 cost and 11 months it took to build demonstrated just how much work was required to give supporters this new home. Sir Stanley Rous performed the opening ceremony before the club's first home league game of the 1961/62 season against Bolton Wanderers. However, plans to adopt similar state-of-the-art stands in other spectator areas were shelved owing to cost. The board could have pushed things through but simply didn't want the sizeable additional expense. Consequently the West or Leppings Lane Stand, which had grown from a small terrace to one of a relatively decent size, was only humbly transformed when compared to the original blueprints. After its complete demolition almost 4,500 seats overlooked a paddocked terraced area. Preparations for the 1966 World Cup inspired its building with work costing £110,000.

BUYING AN ADVANTAGE

Though outlawed now, the practice of selling ground advantage was common for many years. Small Heath had entered many such deals before accepting £200 from The Wednesday to switch their FA Cup second round tie from the Midlands to Sheffield in January 1892. The deal proved to the 'home' side's advantage following a 2–0 win.

INTERNATIONAL SERVICE

Hillsborough has hosted two England internationals. The first, in April 1920, saw just over 25,000 people turn up to watch the home side pip Scotland 5–4 in a thoroughly entertaining game. France were the visitors in October 1962 for a European Nations Cup qualifying match. Ron Springett was the only Wednesday player on duty for the game which finished 1–1.

Northern Ireland have used the ground as an adoptive home. A World Cup qualifying game against Bulgaria in September 1973 was switched from Belfast owing to political troubles. Hillsborough also welcomed participating nations during the 1966 World Cup finals. West Germany, Switzerland, Spain and Argentina played group games in the competition which proved to be England's finest hour. The Germans returned to face Uruguay in a quarter-final tie. Over the course of Euro '96 Portugal, Turkey, Croatia and Denmark set up camp when football came home. The Danes, reigning European champions at the time and second seeds, played all their games at the stadium.

During the Second World War unofficial internationals were held at Hillsborough as well as representative games between a number of leagues. There was also a B international between England and Switzerland in 1950.

LEAGUE

Although not founder members of the Football League, Wednesday were formed many years before most clubs taking part in that competition's initial 1888/89 campaign. Following the move to professionalism and the impressive results Wednesday had already achieved, the club made their first attempt to gain election in time for its second season. However, the original 12 clubs refused a personal application from Wednesday President John Holmes. Many thought a refusal to join those pioneers was held against them. Whatever the reason, election eventually came in 1892 as a result of expansion to two divisions. The top flight took on another four members and Wednesday were elected into one of those spots.

For the most part Wednesday have enjoyed life in the top half of the league structure. The only periods outside the First and Second Division (or equivalents in the Premier League era) came between 1975 and 1980 plus four ad hoc seasons since 2003 until the present day. The 1960s were by far the club's most successful decade within the Football League and based on end-of-season placings, Wednesday had the fifth best record of all 92 league clubs. Only Spurs, Everton, Manchester United and Burnley – all champions over that era – could boast better showings.

It was perhaps fitting that the oldest league club, Notts County – established three years earlier than Wednesday and the Owls' first Football League opposition in the FA Cup – provided the opposition on 3 September 1892 when Wednesday eventually took their bow. In the course of sealing a 1–0 away win, skipper Tom Brandon became the first player to score a league goal. However, it is worth noting that some observers gave the honour to Harry Davis. The line-up for that historic game was Allan, T. Brandon, Mumford, Hall, Betts, H. Brandon, Spiksley, Brady, Davis, R.N. Brown, Dunlop.

As a point of interest, Brandon's only other goal that term came in the return fixture at Hillsborough – the season's last game – when victory spared Wednesday the indignity of a relegation test match. The first league game played at home saw Wednesday entertain Accrington. The Lancashire side were soundly beaten 5–2 at the Olive Grove.

Wednesday's four Football League championships and five Second Division crowns make them one of the most successful teams in terms of claiming divisional titles. A consolidated analysis of their record until May 2011 shows that Wednesday have played 4,406 league games winning 1,682. 1,110 have ended in draws with defeat sustained in 1,614. 6,578 goals have been scored, and 6,392 conceded. This is the twenty-first best record of all league clubs. Wednesday have spent 66 seasons in England's top flight which is the fourteenth best record for residency in the elite rank.

GOALS MEANT JACK ALL

As marksmen go, few compare to the prolific Jack Allen. However, had it not been for an inspired positional change which saw him switch from inside-forward to a more central position, plus a small injury crisis, Hillsborough may never have got the best from this outstanding goal-getter. The former Brentford man was a regular name on the scoresheet in the final few games of the 1927/28 season, notching 4 in 5 outings as the club avoided narrowly relegation after looking like dead certs for the drop. But Jack had to wait until October 1928 to be given an extended run in the side as a result of long-term lay-offs for Ted Harper and Jimmy Trotter. After feeling his way back into form with a single strike against Portsmouth, Allen notched a hat-trick against Birmingham City the following week. Just when it seemed things could get no better he claimed four against Bury. By the spring he had claimed an amazing 22 goals from 14 games which left Wednesday in a great position to take the title. This they duly did, in no small part courtesy of Allan's overall tally of 33 league goals.

A one-season wonder? Far from it. The next term saw him notch 39 league goals including three hat-tricks on the way to a successful defence of the championship. By the time he left for Newcastle United in 1931 he had plundered 85 goals from 114 games with 74 from those two title-winning campaigns – this strike rate of 0.75 was only bettered by Derek Dooley a quarter of a century later. Jack Ball's arrival and subsequent preference to lead the line after a very short dry spell prompted Allen's departure, although it is worth noting that the player was still drawing heavily from the goalscoring well in the Central League when outside the senior team. Allen's first season with the Magpies culminated in an FA Cup win and a goal in the final – albeit a highly controversial one.

WEDNESDAY IN THE FA CUP

1890 – Humbled by Men in Dress Shirts

Wednesday reached a first FA Cup final in 1890, meeting Blackburn Rovers who had to wear formal dress shirts when it was discovered both sides would be playing in blue and white jerseys. A London tailor solved the problem and the Lancastrians looked resplendent as they lifted the cup courtesy of a 6–1 win. That humiliation at the Kennington Oval remains the heaviest defeat inflicted on any club in the showpiece event but 10 years earlier the once-invincible Lancashire outfit were humbled by Wednesday in the club's first FA Cup tie. Not only did the Owls trounce Rovers 4–0, they rubbed salt in an already painful wound by achieving this victory at Ewood Park. Bob Gregory's hat-trick made him hero of the hour. Darwen, near neighbours of Blackburn, checked The Wednesday's progress two rounds later with an emphatic 5–2 win.

A year on from that, in 1882, Wednesday made even greater strides and reached the semi-final. Who should provide the opposition? None other than Blackburn Rovers, who achieved a modicum of revenge posting a 5–1 victory in a replay held at Whalley Bridge, Manchester. Along the way Wednesday notched a few firsts by staging their first ever home FA Cup tie. However, the opening round visitors didn't have far to travel – Sheffield Providence succumbed 2–0. The following round saw Wednesday draw a match for the first time and as a consequence earn the club's first replay. A 2–2 draw in the first meeting was followed by a goalless encounter in the rematch. This was the first time Wednesday had failed to score in an FA Cup match. The second replay held at home ended in an emphatic 5–1 win for Wednesday. One stage later the club recorded a 6–0 win over Upton Park, a record win which only stood until the following year when Spilsby were convincingly dispatched 12–2. Another Sheffield side, Heeley, were up next. The match was also at Sheaf House and ended in victory for the home side by a 3–1 margin.

1896 – Joy at the Palace

The first of three FA Cup wins came six years after disappointment against Blackburn. Wolverhampton Wanderers lined up against the Owls at Crystal Palace. Semi-final berths over the previous two seasons underlined the force Wednesday were beginning to become in the cup, and three of the First Division's eventual top five – Everton, Bolton and Sunderland – had been beaten on the way. Fred Spiksley lost no time in asserting Wednesday's authority by scoring one of the fastest goals in FA Cup final history. Within 60 seconds he collected Archie Brash's throw-in and advanced towards the posts. A sure-fire shot left keeper Billy Tennant clutching at thin air. To this day estimates of its exact timing vary, but the goal remains one of the speediest half-dozen strikes in a final.

Quick-fire scoring was to prove the hallmark of events as the result was completed well before the interval. David Black replied 7 minutes after Wolves went behind, but just past the quarter of an hour mark Spiksley restored the advantage with a thunderous shot which hit the crossbar then netting so hard that it actually bounced back into play. The Wanderers' keeper didn't actually realise a goal had been scored until told so by a team-mate and then Wednesday skipper Jack Earp. In fairness to the custodian he had been injured during the build-up. This time Wednesday hung on to their lead and Earp was presented with the freshly minted trophy to the joy of the travelling Wednesday fans. Back home, supporters at Midland station further exhibited their delight. Although good natured, many thousands packed the platforms a full hour before their heroes' 5.28 p.m. arrival time leaving police powerless to maintain order and forcing the players to parade their trophy amid scenes of chaos as the cup came not only to Sheffield but Yorkshire for the first time.

1907 – Late drama secures tight win

In 1906 Everton put Wednesday out of the FA Cup in a dramatic quarter-final tie. That narrow 4–3 win proved to be all the inspiration the Merseysiders needed as they went on to lift the trophy. The two met once more just over 12 months later in a straight battle for silverware. Despite moderate league form, the Owls dispatched Wolves, Southampton, Sunderland, Liverpool and Woolwich Arsenal without too many problems; then emerged triumphant courtesy of a 2–1 scoreline at Crystal Palace. Jimmy Stewart opened the scoring on 21 minutes only for Jack Sharp – the match winner 12 months earlier – to equalise just before half time. Things remained tight throughout the second period but George Simpson won the FA Cup for Wednesday in the most dramatic fashion with a late strike after Andrew Wilson found him unmarked, Simpson heading past a helpless Billy Scott.

1935 – Emphatic at the Empire Stadium

There were more late heroics in the Owls' first Wembley FA Cup Final. Ellis Rimmer's exploits paved the road to the Twin Towers in 1935. The winger scored 6 goals during the run including at least 1 in every round. Any Wednesday fans expecting further heroism in the final were not disappointed as Rimmer notched 2 in as many minutes in a 4–2 victory. The Baggies possessed some of the period's most feared strikers and two very decent wingmen who created sufficient clear-cut chances, but found themselves playing catch-up as Wednesday took the lead twice only to be pegged back. Jack Palethorpe and Mark Hooper scored the other Wednesday goals. However, this was as complete a team performance as had been witnessed in a final.

Albion's Wally Boyes, a boyhood Owl and proud Sheffield lad, equalised Palethorpe's second-minute opener and Teddy Sandford, who would eventually join Sheffield United, replied to Mark Hooper's second. Soon after, a limping Joe Carter struck an upright; it was a let off Rimmer took full advantage of. Supporters who gained one of just a limited number of tickets made available to Wednesdayites had their applications picked out of a hat by two people from Sheffield's Royal Institute for the Blind. Despite the national stadium's capacity being well over 90,000, the amount earmarked for Hillsborough fans was in a derisory four figures.

1966 – Not you again!

Blackburn Rovers are not the only team Wednesday have fought out some epic FA Cup battles with. Although the draw is a completely random event it seems certain teams are regularly paired with each other. Everton also fit into that category. After four minutes of their meeting in the 1966 final Jim McAlliog became one of the youngest players to score an FA Cup final goal at a mere 19 years and 234 days old (although it is worth noting that a headed deflection by Toffees' left-back Ray Wilson threw a cloud over this claim). When David Ford doubled the advantage just before the hour mark it seemed Wednesday were home and dry.

It is possible the euphoria got to the players as Mike Trebilcock pulled one back within 60 seconds – the Merseysiders were back in the game but all Wednesday had to do was keep their heads and concentration up. However, five minutes later the same player levelled affairs. A pitch invasion followed as jubilant Evertonians expressed their disbelief. One particular supporter – Eddie Kavanagh – evaded many attempts to apprehend his joyous trot across the hallowed turf, even slipping out of his suit jacket when he seemed cornered.

The game had a completely different flavour now and as Everton pushed forward the Owls' defence fell apart. Derek Temple capitalised on a terrible blunder by Gerry Young just 10 minutes from the end which left Ron Springett exposed. Young's devastated reaction summed up the mood. With that kind of spirit there could be no way back.

That final was one of the most remarkable in recent history and is still talked about by many fans – not just of the teams involved. Wednesday had taken the tricky route to Wembley, playing away in every round. Such was the Owls' contribution to a classic game that they became the first team to do a losers' lap of honour on the final whistle. Up to the close of the 2010/11 season Wednesday had drawn Everton

14 times – playing 19 games. An Everton win is the most common result in these encounters as Wednesday have lost 9 and won just 5, the last victory being in February 1954.

1993 – Oh brother!

Wednesday's first FA Cup final in more than a quarter of a century went to a replay. The Owls had finished seventh in the debut Premier League season which contrasted favourably to Arsenal's tenth spot. However, the two sides had already contested domestic silverware with the Gunners winning the League Cup by the odd goal in three. Five weeks on from that game there was a chance for revenge, though Wednesday went behind to an Ian Wright goal during the opening quarter. David Hirst equalised just past the hour with extra time unable to separate two well-matched teams.

Wright netted the opener when the sides met again. Chris Waddle managed to square matters with a low shot which found the net via Lee Dixon. However, Arsenal scored in the last minute of injury time. A penalty shoot-out was beckoning and set to decide an FA Cup winner for the first time. Though few fancied that lottery, Wednesday fans may have preferred that to watching Andy Linighan heading in from a corner. Chris Woods got his fingers to the ball but as Graham Hyde attempted to clear, he could only help it in. Linighan was nursing a broken nose after being elbowed square in the face by Mark Bright – who he out-jumped to reach the corner. Additionally, his younger brother, Brian, was on the Hillsborough books. The then teenager made his only Owls appearances the following season.

AT THE THIRD TIME OF ASKING

After hammering Notts County 5–0 in the 1889/90 FA Cup quarter-final, Wednesday seemed to have booked an easy passage to the last four. However, County's officials felt the pitch didn't meet minimum standards and this had proved a major factor in their defeat. The FA upheld their complaint. After the restaged meeting it was Wednesday who cried foul. County had won 3–2 but with the aid of an ineligible player. Again the powers that be held an inquiry and found in favour of the complainant. The third game, a tense affair, was won by The Wednesday 2–1 and without any objections. Soon after, the FA decided it would only hear grievances registered before games.

Disposing of Bolton Wanderers in the next stage meant Wednesday became the first club to reach a final after not just losing an FA Cup game but having been eliminated. Only Charlton Athletic can equal part of this claim. They lost a game when cup matches were played over two legs the first season after the Second World War finished. Wednesday have a proud record of competing in each FA Cup competition since 1880 bar one. In 1886/87 the club were forced to sit it out after submitting their entry beyond the closing date.

TWO WINS ON ONE DAY

In 1898, dark November lived up to its name when bad light forced the abandonment of a Division One game between Wednesday and Aston Villa after 79 minutes. The game at Owlerton had kicked off 7 minutes late as referee, Mr Aaron Scragg, had missed his train from Manchester by a mere 10 seconds. Local official Fred Bye took charge until the interval.

At the time it was usual for a remaining period to be played at a later date rather than start the game from scratch. Wednesday claimed their 3–1 advantage would have been too much for Villa to overhaul but the encounter was played to a finish just under four months later on 13 March 1899. Villa returned to Sheffield in order to see out a mere 11 minutes of a match they trailed in by two goals. Both teams fielded slightly differing sides than in the original tie. Wednesday added an extra goal but in order to give full value to the 3,000 fans who turned up, a full-scale friendly between the sides was arranged. 35 minutes were played each way with gate money going to Harry Davis. For the record the Owls won 2–0.

A LICK OF PAINT

During the Edwardian era players were expected to be a hardy bunch. There was no talk of health and safety for fans or those they came to watch. Back then games could be played on a good few inches of snow and after making sure the lines were visible, a home game with Coventry City on Boxing Day was allowed to take place after both goal frames were painted a rather fetching shade of dark blue.

THROUGH ON AGGREGATE

Only League Cup and European ties are regularly contested over two legs although the season after professional football returned to normal following the Second World War, FA Cup matches were decided on the same basis until the semi-final stage. The experiment was scrapped after just one season but Wednesday would still do well to beat the 11–2 record set against York City in the fourth round.

In the League Cup a 10–0 thrashing of Stockport County in September 1986 set a competition record. It included a 7–0 win at Maine Road which acted as the Cheshire club's temporary home and allowed them to maximise the gate revenue. Spora Luxembourg are the only side Wednesday have managed to post double figures against in Europe. The 10–2 hammering of the part-timers came in the first round of the 1992/93 UEFA Cup campaign.

ALL-ROUNDERS

Tom Armitage and George Ulyett played for both the Wednesday cricket and football clubs. Each also represented Yorkshire and made history by playing for England in the world's very first Test match against Australia in March 1877 at the Melbourne Cricket Ground. Armitage has the dubious honour of dropping the first catch in Test cricket – Charles Bannerman off Alfred Shaw's bowling. Ullyett's contribution was to force a dominant Bannerman to retire hurt on 165 after a wickedly delivered bouncer split the index finger of his right hand.

Alongside club and international representation William Clegg turned out for Oxford University many times, although perhaps Frank Sugg was the ultimate sportsman. A stylish right-handed batsmen as well as occasional wicket-keeper at county and international level, he was one of *Wisden*'s prestigious Cricketers of the Year in 1890. During the winter he played for Derby County, Burnley, The Wednesday, Bolton Wanderers and Everton – the latter being the only club he represented in the Football League. Suggs was an immense man with great strength fully utilised in both sports. This also allowed him to partake in weightlifting and putting the shot. Those muscles provided enough stamina to make him a consummate long-distance swimmer. Suggs also excelled in sports requiring more finesse, such as billiards and rifle shooting.

Don Megson took one of the most diverse steps by trying his hand at American Football while playing soccer across the Atlantic. John Fantham is said to have been both an exceptional cricketer and golfer who could just as easily taken up either of those sports professionally.

THE ITALIAN JOBS

As a Third Division team, 1968/69 League Cup winners Swindon Town were not allowed to play in the following season's Fairs Cup – the usual reward for their victory. Some recompense came in a two-legged encounter with Coppa Italia winners AS Roma. The Wiltshire side recorded an unlikely victory and also drew a huge crowd to the County Ground. To give lower division sides a chance to earn a little extra finance by playing continental opposition, the Anglo-Italian Cup was born.

Wednesday only participated in the inaugural tournament held at the close of the 1969/70 season but were able to pit their wits against Napoli and Juventus. Both group games were played over two legs. Wednesday beat Napoli 4–3 at home but were brought back down to earth by a 5–1 defeat in Italy. Juventus also triumphed in their own back yard 2–0, although the Owls did hold the Turin giants to a goalless draw back in Yorkshire.

IN ORDER OF APPEARANCE

Andy Wilson's place as the only man to have made more than 500 league outings for Wednesday seems secure for many years to come. With fewer players spending a great length of time at clubs it may never be broken. 43 appearances in cup games bolster the striker's tally of 502 to 545 overall between 1900 and 1920.

The top 10 appearance makers in all competition for the club are as follows:

Andy Wilson	545
Jack Brown	507
Alan Finney	503
Kevin Pressman	478
Tommy Crawshaw	465
Redfern Froggatt	458
Don Megson	442
John Fantham	426 (9)
Ernie Blenkinshop	424
Teddy Davison	424

Fifteen players have made 100 or more consecutive appearances for Wednesday. In common with most clubs, goalkeepers tend to dominate, with four representatives including Martin Hodge who holds the record courtesy of the 214 games he played on the spin from 27 August 1983 to 31 August 1987. However, Mark Hooper played more consecutive league games during his run dating between 6 April 1928 and 23 April 1932. Over his 36 months at Hillsborough Lee Grant missed just one game.

Other members of this exclusive club are:

Mark Hooper	189
Hugh Swift	140
Horace Burrows	136
Lee Grant	136
Bob Bolder	133
Don Megson	129
Ellis Rimmer	117
Jimmy Campbell	116
Richard Walden	110
Frank Westlake	110
Peter Johnson	104
Teddy Davison	101
Tony Kay	101
Harry Ruddlesdin	100

MANAGING THE OWLS

From the day the Owls were formed until just after the First World War the club had never appointed a manager, preferring to leave control of team affairs in the hands of the club secretary Arthur Dickinson who made his decisions in conjunction with the board. There seemed little impetus for change as during his reign – lasting from August 1891 to May 1920 – Wednesday won two League Championships and the FA Cup. He remains the longest-serving of 31 Wednesday managers – that figure includes caretakers. Relegation from Division One proved the catalyst for the club's first formal appointment of a team manager, Bob Brown, who resigned as Gillingham boss after just four weeks at the helm in order to take the role. Although he too combined secretarial duties with footballing matters, Brown was in sole charge of the players and tactics. The change proved beneficial. His tenure lasted 13 years with a Second Division title and two League Championships secured over that spell.

Of the managers to succeed Brown, only Eric Taylor (who also acted as a secretary/manager) has spent longer in the hotseat – although his time was punctuated by the Second World War.

Peter Eustace's 4 months in charge has been the shortest time any permanent manager has stayed in post at Hillsborough. Those to have shorter reigns are Rob Kelly who was temporarily installed for 24 hours prior to Gary Megson replacing Alan Irvine in February 2011. Bill Green had six days in caretaker charge and Sean McAuley held a similar status for a fortnight. Peter Shreeves had three spells as a caretaker. The latter was extended to six months, half of which he served as boss in his own right when the 2000/01 season ended. He won the right to that permanent role by ensuring Wednesday were saved from the drop and scooping March's Manager of the Month award. However, after a poor start to the next season, he resigned.

Eustace, Derek Dooley, Howard Wilkinson, Trevor Francis, Chris Turner, Danny Wilson and Gary Megson are the only Wednesday players to have also managed the club. Scotsmen Jimmy McMullan, Paul Sturrock and Alan Irvine plus Terry Yorath, who represented Wales during his playing days, are the only non-English managers. Although Danny Wilson represented Northern Ireland, he was born in Wigan.

BIG RON

Excluding those drafted in temporarily, Ron Atkinson is the only manager to have two stints at the club. Wednesday have employed a wide variety of bosses but perhaps none have been as flamboyant as 'Big Ron'. The removal of Peter

Eustace just months before the close of the 1988/89 campaign left a void the Hillsborough executives knew they had to fill with the right man if good times were to return. Before that could happen, the first job was to save the Owls from top-flight relegation. It proved to be mission impossible but never one to be daunted by a task, Ron rubbed the magic lamp to release the genie that seemed to have guided him for most of his managerial career. Wednesday not only bounced back to Division One at the first time of asking but recorded a deserved victory over Manchester United in the 1991 League Cup final – the club's first major trophy success for 56 years.

A few months after tasting Wembley glory, Atkinson left to take charge of Aston Villa. Speculation had mounted over many weeks prompting a pledge to stay at Wednesday not long before he left. Many fans were incensed by his betrayal but were forced to make their peace in November 1997 when, faced with the threat of relegation again, a hard-pressed board felt compelled to call on Ron once more. Armed with a contract until the end of the season and a cheque book, the task at hand was to keep Wednesday clear of the drop zone. Owls' chairman Dave Richards was keen to point out the seemingly bizarre rationale behind the decision saying, 'I know Ron Atkinson regretted some of the things he did but he has had a wonderful love affair with Wednesday. We need his experience now.'

If there was one manager capable of falling head first into the compost heap yet still come up smelling of roses it was Ron. Typically he picked the most opportune time for a hate figure to make a triumphant return. It may have been a close squeak but given the dire straits the Owls were in, landing 4 points clear of trouble was cause for celebration. The reward of a long-term contract was expected but just a week after completing the rescue mission Ron found himself on the receiving end of a sucker punch. Though happy to stay on, the near 60-year-old suggested it should only be for 12 months. Planning for the future was key to Wednesday, who opted to look elsewhere.

HIGHS & LOWS

Hillsborough played host to the 49,309 fans who set a record for a game in the third tier of English football (since the North and South divisions were dispensed with). They came to watch a Sheffield derby played on 26 December 1979 but even that figure is dwarfed by the record 72,841 fans who packed the ground to see the fifth round FA Cup encounter with Manchester City in February 1934. The Blades were the opposition when Hillsborough's record league attendance was set – 65,384 spectators witnessed the clash in January 1952.

Bolton Wanderers' visit during the 1932/33 First Division campaign failed to capture the imagination given the disappointing 4,810 crowd which filed through the gates. This is the lowest attendance for any home league game at the ground since it became known as Hillsborough. Under its former guise of Owlerton the lowest crowd was a mere 2,500 for a match against Everton in April 1902.

BOTH SIDES OF THE CITY

Thirty-eight players have been on the books of both the Owls and Blades as either fully fledged signings or part of loan deals. Bernard Oxby's transfer to Wednesday in May 1934 was the first between the clubs since the twentieth century began. It ended a 35-year moratorium on recruiting each other's players. Alan Quinn is the only man to score for both clubs in derby games and the most recent to make a direct switch – in the summer of 2004. Walter Rickett started his career with Sheffield United scoring on his debut – one of the few players to have done so with his first touch. In a strange twist of fate, the opposition that day were Wednesday. He atoned for his sins joining the Owls in October 1949; who he helped claim two Second Division championships during the early part of the 1950s.

Imre Varadi played for both sides but never made an outing in a Steel City derby. Ben Wilkinson, son of former Hillsborough boss Howard, signed up for Wednesday's academy but was allowed to leave whereon he entered the same set-up at Bramall Lane. Wilkinson senior served with Sheffield United over a number of seasons but failed to emerge beyond the Central League before joining Wednesday with whom he finally made a breakthrough to senior football. Bob Barnshaw, a centre-half who caught Wednesday's eye during a scouting mission to the North-East left the Owls for the Blades but failed to represent either in a senior game before joining Southern League Watford.

For some, the prospect of turning out with both Wednesday and United proved nothing more than a rumour. There was talk of Redfern Froggatt joining Sheffield United once he slipped out of the first-team picture at Wednesday, but he decided to stay and managed to regain his place. There was artistic license in Mel Sterland and Charlie Williamson's fictional defections to the Blades. Both played Sheffield United players in the film *When Saturday Comes*. Each served a few clubs after leaving Wednesday, but Bramall Lane was not among their stops.

Not only players have found themselves straddling both sides of the divide. Charles Stokes was an original member of the Wednesday committee but subsequently became a founder of Sheffield United. Derek Dooley played for and managed the Owls then served the Blades as a commercial manager among other roles before becoming managing director then chairman of United's football club board. Sam Ellis had almost three years as assistant manager at Bramall Lane in December 2010, leaving a short while after Kevin Blackwell was dismissed.

To little acclaim from fans, Danny Wilson took the Sheffield United manager's job in May 2011. Former Wednesday keeper Teddy Davison never played for United but did manage the club between 1932 and 1952, while Ian Porterfield is another former Owl to have taken charge of team affairs at Bramall Lane. He spent three years at Hillsborough from 1977, but within 12 months of leaving he was starting the tough job of rebuilding the Blades' shattered ambitions. This he duly did leading them from the Fourth to Second Division in just three seasons before being sacked. Former captain Jack Hudson, who pulled on the red and white stripes later in his career, is another to have joined the coaching staff at Bramall Lane. Boyhood Owl Mark Smith had a lengthy career as a player at Hillsborough and returned once his playing days were over to work in the academy. Chris Turner's departure in 2004 saw him installed as caretaker-manager for a defeat by Coventry City before a return to his old role. A restructure of the junior set-up left him without a job just a couple of years later and open to an offer to become Sheffield United's International Youth Director. He has since taken other jobs below senior level.

Here's the full list of players to have appeared for both teams:.

Carl Bradshaw	David Ford	Derek Geary
Leigh Bromby	Oliver Tummon	James Harrop
Franz Carr	Dean Windass	Jack Hudson
Joe Cockroft	Carl Robinson	David Johnson
Terry Curran	Lance Key	Tommy Johnson

Jeff King	Billy Mellors	Walter Rickett
Imre Varadi	Billy Mosforth	Wilf Rostron
Earl Barrett	Bernard Oxley	Bernard Shaw
Danny Batth	George Walker	Simon Stainrod
Chris Marsden	Alan Quinn	Charles Taylor
Brian Marwood	Owen Morrison	Alan Warboys
Jon-Paul	Richard Cresswell	Walter Rickett
McGovern	Neil Ramsbottom	Paul Heald

BATTH TIMES FOR OWLS & BLADES

Playing for both Sheffield clubs in the same season is not a unique feat – but doing so on loan is. Danny Batth appeared for Wednesday and United during the 2010/11 season on this basis. Each side took him on emergency terms from Wolverhampton Wanderers outside the transfer window. The Blades had him for a month just ahead of Christmas while the promising centre-back joined Wednesday from March until the campaign ended. The following July Wolves allowed a six-month temporary transfer back to Hillsborough.

WAR RATIONS

The peculiar circumstances of both world wars saw Wednesday and United share many players, and quite often over the same season. During the First World War these included Harold Bell, Ernest Blackwell, J.W. Booth, Charles Brelsford, Harold Buddery, Tom Cawley, S. Ford, Joseph Godfrey, Jimmy Harrop, Percy Oldacre, A. Price, Harold Salt, H. Spratt and Oliver Tummon. Slightly fewer were able to make the same kind of switches during the next conflict with only Harold Barton, Alf Calverley, Bob Curry, Ken Gadsbury, Tom Johnson, George Laking, Walter Millership, Jack Smith, Hugh Swift and Fred White wearing the shirts of both sides.

FATHER UNLIKE SON

Matt Barrass, a half-back turned forward from the North-East, who enjoyed just over a season at Hillsborough, had a son named Malcolm, born in Blackpool during December 1924. This was just over four months before his father's stay at Wednesday ended, an offer from Manchester City proved too tempting for the Owls to resist after his first full season. Malcolm later became a professional with Bolton Wanderers who he won international honours with and reached the famous 1953 'Matthews' Final'. However, on leaving Burnden Park he joined Sheffield United.

THE EARL OF SHEFFIELD

Although not traded between the two clubs, six days after turning out for the Blades, Earl Barrett was making an Owls debut. The England international had spent five weeks on loan at United from Everton during the 1997/98 season gaining first-team football during an injury-plagued few years. Courtesy of his contribution to United the defender was offered terms by Sheffield Wednesday who had watched his progress keenly. So, effectively 48 hours after officially leaving Bramall Lane, he was being photographed at Hillsborough on completing a free transfer. Sadly more fitness setbacks ended his career in 2000.

ON SECOND THOUGHTS

A cold snap in January 1947 possibly averted one of the most shocking defections between the Sheffield clubs. Dugald Livingstone was a well-respected and highly successful trainer at Bramall Lane but when Wednesday decided to appoint a team manager rather than leave all decisions in the hands of secretary/manager Eric Taylor, the Scotsman sought the chance to gain extra responsibility. He applied for and accepted the post. The news was announced on 20 January 1947 but prior to Wednesday playing again – weather caused postponements until 2 February – Livingstone decided he could not go through with the switch and opted to remain with the Blades. Though he left Bramall Lane soon after, he had a decent managerial career elsewhere supervising club and international sides. Meanwhile, Taylor remained in post for an additional 11 years.

ROVING EYES

Although Sheffield Rovers never kicked a ball in anger they could very well have proved to be Wednesday's most potent enemy and radically changed the city's footballing history. When football was in its infancy, teams were not allowed to field professionals, even though indirectly funding those who wore the club's colours was common practice. Wednesday kept to the letter of the law if not always the spirit, a case in point being Scottish player James Lang who was recruited in 1876 and, while never paid by the club, he was employed by a firm owned by a Wednesday board member.

The late return of entry papers for the 1886/87 FA Cup caused a rethink about amateurism as a number of players

– including Tom Cawley and Billy Mosforth – decided to turn out for an entrant who did complete their paperwork. Lockwood Brothers were a team formed by workers at a Sheffield factory of the same name. The experience could have sounded the death knell for Wednesday as many of their players decided to form their own professional club called Sheffield Rovers. The real prospect of losing their entire squad led to urgent talks being sought with the rebels and their negotiator-in-chief Mosforth. Despite some initial protestations by a number of players, peace was called on 22 April 1887 thanks in no small part to an impassioned plea by Cawley. The Wednesday board decided the club should go professional and paid their players 5s for home games and 7s 6d for away matches. Extra money was made available for attending training for sessions. Cawley was one of the first to backtrack once the club tried to build bridges and persuaded his colleagues to return.

THE ULTIMATE FOOTBALL MERCENARY

There is constant criticism and debate about mercenary attitudes of players within the modern game but even today's professional would have struggled to keep up with the record of the aforementioned Billy Mosforth. The lack of a contract-based system of player recruitment during the 1870s left him free to play for whichever club took his fancy. This would include a couple at the same time and quite often he would turn out for both Wednesday and Sheffield Albion on the same day. Only when the two met did he have to make a choice. Such was his prowess that on one occasion when Wednesday were due to face Albion, Owls fans offered him cash to change sides. The offer was readily taken up and moments before kick-off allegiances were switched. Wednesday tied him down in 1877 but in the best traditions of the early part of his career, he left in 1889 to join United.

Bramall Lane may have been his last port of call but Mosforth also served Sheffield Rovers, Hallam and Sheffield Zulus. Although a very different beast from Mosforth, Jack Hunter was another local man to spread himself around the city's clubs with Sheffield Heeley, Providence, Sheffield Albion and the Zulus on his CV.

MARATHON MEN

Wednesday's longest cup tie by far was the FA Cup third round encounter with Arsenal in 1979. The Owls were at their lowest ebb having spent four complete seasons in Division Three, while the Gunners were the previous year's FA Cup semi-finalists. The first game at Hillsborough went ahead only after a Herculean effort to clear snow and ice was undertaken by groundsmen and a large number of fans. It finished 1–1, Jeff Johnson writing himself in to the headlines by scoring the goal, an equaliser to Alan Sunderland's early strike. Although it seemed the Owls' best chance of an upset had gone, the Highbury replay saw the underdogs hold on for the same result. This time Rodger Wylde was on target and was set to win the tie until Liam Brady squared matters in the closing minute.

Three further replays all held at Leicester City's Filbert Street (owing to its ability to stave off freezing temperatures) were needed to decide matters. Former Gunner Brian Hornsby turned on his former employers in the next game which finished 2–2 by scoring both goals including a penalty. He was on the mark once more in the next match 48 hours later – again from the spot, although this time as a match-saver during extra time. David Rushbury and John Lowey had scored inside the regulation 90 minutes. Arsenal eventually made it through courtesy of a 2–0 win in the fifth and final game the teams had contested in 17 days.

The total played time amounted to a mammoth (not to mention competition record) 9½ hours. With the Owls needing a second bite in each of the first two rounds, 900 minutes – 15 hours – were spent in FA Cup action that term.

CENTENARY CELEBRATIONS

Wednesday celebrated their centenary by allowing fans to attend the home league game scheduled after their founding date for half the usual price. Wednesday ran out 4–2 winners over Fulham but only 26,551 spectators attended. Given the financial incentive it seems strange that games with Leicester City and Burnley played in the preceding fortnight attracted more supporters. The Owls celebrated their 100th birthday – 4 September 1967 – as league leaders courtesy of a 1–0 away win at Bramall Lane 48 hours earlier. However, relegation was narrowly avoided by the season's end as Wednesday finished nineteenth in the final analysis.

Talking of centenaries, Wednesday have scored 100 times or more in a number of seasons, including 105 in the course of securing the 1929/30 championship. During the 1955/56 title-winning season, 101 goals were scored. A few years earlier during the 1951/52, exactly 100 were scored and seven years later in 1958/59 an aggregate of 106 was achieved. Wednesday won the Second Division championship on both of these occasions but were relegated from Division One when precisely 100 goals were put past their defence in 1954/55.

AWAY DAYS

Owls teams have posted many great victories away from home the best being in the League Cup when Aldershot were beaten 8–0 on 3 October 1989. In other competitions the record wins are as follows:

Premiership	West Ham United	4–0	16 January 1999
Football League	Nottingham Forest	6–0	23 April 1910
	West Ham United	6–0	8 December 1951
FA Cup	Manchester United	7–2	1 February 1961

The 1898/99, 1900/01, 1926/27, 1957/58 and 1975/76 campaigns were by far the worst travelling vintage of any Wednesday side – the Owls went each of those entire league campaigns without a win. On the brighter side Wednesday won 11 of the 21 away games played on the way to the 1929/30 championship.

RISKING GOD'S WRATH

Alec Brady, a signing from Celtic in 1892, was a man Wednesday risked invoking the wrath of God for. At least that would have been the course of events if the Roman Catholic priest who followed the inside-forward down from Scotland had got his way. The story goes that when Brady and his colleague Jack Madden reported for their trials, this soccer-loving man of the cloth attempted to stop any proposed transfer and take the duo home. Both players went into hiding but Madden was found and forced to return. Brady proved altogether better at these cloak-and-dagger operations, managing to avoid detection then going on to score a hat-trick on debut. He left Wednesday in January 1899 after almost 200 league and cup outings.

FIGHT CLUB

Scotland was fertile hunting ground for clubs just before the twentieth century commenced. Almost every English side had scouts operating north of the border and were able to pay far higher sums than any of their counterparts across Hadrian's Wall. Such opportunities were usually seized upon by players and two whom Wednesday had cast greedy eyes on – Dumbarton pair Spiers and Towie – were contacted then presented with terms by a high-level party dispatched from South Yorkshire.

Negotiations were held in a restaurant but took time as neither player was so keen that they put pen to paper immediately. Though Towie was eventually persuaded to sign on the dotted line, Spiers was far more reticent. Not only that, the location proved to be a mistake as local players talking to well-heeled Englishmen aroused suspicion and word filtered back to Boghead Park officials who confronted the diners. More than heated words were exchanged as a couple of men, who seemed more comfortable with hand-to-hand combat than earnest conciliation, had been recruited by the Scottish club to get their players back. Those credentials were immediately on display; crockery went flying and tables were upturned with the Wednesday party trying to fight their way out rather than confront their would-be assailants. Eventually they managed to beat a hasty if bloodied retreat while the would-be quarry stayed with the Sons.

ON THE BALL

A close-season signing from Manchester United in 1930, Jack Ball had one of the most prolific records of any pre-war striker. He scored 17 goals in his first 14 Wednesday games including hat-tricks against Sunderland and Leicester City. Although the prolific scoring waned a little, Ball still finished that first campaign with 27 goals from the 36 league appearances made. In just over three seasons he hit 94 goals from 135 appearances – many in the final minutes. That tally was bolstered by penalties but was still a record to be proud of. His best season by far was the 1932/33 campaign when he grabbed 35 strikes from 42 league and cup outings. Ball returned to Old Trafford in exchange for Neil Dewar at Christmas 1933.

BACK TO FRONT

Paul Warhurst was signed as a dependable centre-half able to play across the backline but was utilised as an emergency striker when Mark Bright and David Hirst were laid low by injuries during the spring of 1993. After scoring 12 goals in as many games – primarily in the cups – he earned an England call-up in the role. Unfortunately a groin injury prevented the chance of a first, and as it would have turned out only, senior cap. Trevor Francis's insistence that he return to preventing goals rather than scoring them led to some unrest and attention from other clubs, including Blackburn Rovers who had essentially become the highest-spending club in England. Their accepted £2.7 million offer realised a three-and-a-half-fold profit on Wednesday's original investment but more groin problems plus bad breaks to each leg saw Blackburn's hopes of a pairing with Alan Shearer frustrated. When another converted defender, Chris Sutton, was brought to Ewood Park, Warhurst largely returned to the position he broke through in as a youngster.

BACK-TO-BACK CHAMPIONS

Wednesday beat Aston Villa and Sunderland by a single point to win their first league championship in 1903 but effectively saw destiny removed from their hands while occupying top spot. The Owls had wrapped up their campaign with Sunderland still to settle their last game of the season – a derby against Newcastle United. The Magpies were two places clear of the relegation zone but mathematically safe. As a consequence most people expected the Wearsiders to win through. However, Newcastle pulled off an unlikely victory and sealed Wednesday's crown. The champions were playing a friendly in Plymouth at the time but had half an eye on events 300 miles north. The following season Wednesday retained their crown although this time there was no edge-of-the-seat finale. Runners-up Manchester City trailed by three points.

Wednesday became one of the few sides to win back-to-back titles twice, in 1930 although in the first of these seasons (1928/29) victory was just as tight as their debut success. Leicester City were pipped to the post by a single point when they failed to beat Huddersfield Town while Wednesday drew at Burnley. Success had been built on a number of resounding home performances as away form was less than optimum. However, 12 months later the Owls defended their prize in scintillating fashion ending ten points clear of Derby County.

FOR STARTERS

Fifteen games without defeat constitutes Wednesday's best ever start to a campaign. This run came at the opening of the 1983/84 season when 11 games were won and 4 drawn.

Crystal Palace became the first team to beat the Owls with a 1–0 victory on 26 November. Goal difference saw Wednesday lose out on the Second Division title to a free-scoring Chelsea but achieve promotion to the top flight as runners-up.

ALSO KNOWN AS

Although often referred to as Wednesday the club's only nickname these days is the Owls. However, Wednesday actually carried the Blades as their epithet until moving to Owlerton. The city's main industry and use of steel to make cutting implements led to this nickname being extended to most if not all Sheffield teams at one time or another; though for a while United would always be referred to as the Cutlers. This was another generic title bestowed on the city's teams and again a steel-related nickname. To distinguish United and Wednesday further, the latter were known as the Grovites while they were playing at Olive Grove and United were referred to as Laneites.

Though residency in the Owlerton district played a part in Sheffield Wednesday's alternative moniker it only gained real currency after the presentation of a wooden owl by then outside-left George Robertson to the club in October 1912. The figure – a gift in honour of the stadium – was placed up in the North Stand rafters and its presence coincided with a decent run of home form.

IRISH BAIL-OUT

Scottish international George Robertson, a school teacher during the week, had something of a liking for mementos. On one occasion this nearly led to trouble. After his nation beat Ireland 2–1 at Dalymount Park through a late and controversial Alec Bennett goal, they avoided the 1913 British Home Championship's wooden spoon. A host of Scottish players tried to grab the ball. It led to something of a mêlée which Robertson emerged victorious from. Spectators got involved including Irishman Patrick Gartland who knocked the prize from the Wednesday player's hands. Right-half Billy Andrews claimed it back but a scuffle began from which Gartland was left with a broken leg.

Rumour quickly spread that Robertson was the perpetrator of that injury and some local fans set about trying to gain redress. Changing room windows were smashed which kept the visiting team within the poky confines of their retreat for more than a hour. Police eventually went in and arrested the winger. The Irish FA stepped in to agree financial recompense for the injured supporter who in return dropped his complaint. That didn't stop some and a mob followed the Scotland squad to their hotel remonstrating further. Full-back Jock Walker was attacked. Out of custody Robertson beat a quick and relieved retreat back to Sheffield.

A DELVE INTO THE KIT BAG

For most of their history Wednesday have proudly worn broad blue and white stripes as their first-choice kit, but Owls' teams have also played in squares and hoops. A blue jersey was used for just one game in March 1935. During the late 1960s and early 1970s they wore blue shirts with white sleeves. The first Wednesday team took to the field in blue shirts with white trims, before then favouring blue and white quarters. Both jerseys were accompanied by white shorts. In the 1870s blue and white hoops were worn but this design was a short-lived innovation which only made a brief return after the Second World War.

On election to the Football League stripes were the preferred choice but with blue shorts and shades of this colour and black have been the preferred accompaniment. There were few changes in the post-war period until those blue shirts with white sleeves and neck trim were teamed up with white shorts – a look very similar in style to Arsenal's strip around the same period. Two years after they were adopted, those shirts were dropped and replaced by the traditional stripes. Dark shorts also returned to the kit bag. Bold stripes were temporarily replaced by a pinstripe design in 1987 but returned a year later. As kit manufacturers tried differentiating their offerings to supporters in more recent times, a bib-like blue band ran straight down the front with an uninterrupted white backdrop. This lasted just a couple of seasons from which time the basic principle of white and blue stripes has remained.

Styles of change strips have varied as has the number of colours. The most memorable combinations include green shirts with blue hoops plus green shorts and socks. Green and white have also been combined. So has yellow with a blue trim and then yellow with slender black stripes, not to mention virtually solid black. Wednesday played in all white during the 1966 FA Cup run and have adopted this as a change strip since along with other racy combinations such as plain orange then the same colour with white. There have been sober greys – in the mid-1980s this was mixed with a rather fetching lilac.

THE SILK ROAD TO WEMBLEY

When Wednesday reached their fourth FA Cup final in 1935 the club opted to mark the occasion with silk shirts rather than the usual woollen mix teams usually had. The bespoke tailoring came at no small cost but the jersey was too big for the diminutive Mark Hooper whose spindly frame, said to weigh less than the 10 stones of a super-lightweight boxer, simply couldn't gain any purchase from the smooth natural fibres. He had to be given one of the non-commemorative kits – the white away shirt fortunately packed before the players left Yorkshire – but that meant all Owls' players selected needed to change out of the more luxurious outfits. At least there was recompense in the final result and with the aid of a post, Hooper grabbed one of the goals in a 4–2 win over West Bromwich Albion.

PUTTING THEIR SHIRTS ON WEDNESDAY

During the summer of 2000 Wednesday announced their biggest shirt sponsorship with confectionery makers Chupa Chups worth £1 million over two years. It replaced a deal with Sanderson Electronics. Other companies to have literally put the shirts on Wednesday's back are Crosby Kitchens, MHS, Finlux, VT Plastics, Diadora, Mr Tom, Napoleons Casino and PlusNet Broadband. ASDA signed a one-match deal for the 1991 League Cup final.

Sponsorship was donated to Sheffield Children's Hospital throughout the 2009/10 and 2010/11 seasons. Wednesday's links with this worthwhile cause have been lengthy – prior to this act of corporate altruism Hillsborough legend David Hirst donated 30 per cent of proceeds from his testimonial to hospital funds. During the 2009/10 season the 125th Steel

City derby saw the teams share the duty of promoting the hospital. This was for one match only although both Sheffield clubs will share sponsors for the 2011/12 term. Local Volkswagen dealership, Gilders, and Westfield Health agreed a joint deal so as not to appear partisan. Wednesday will wear the Gilders branding on home shirts with Westfield Health on change strips while the Blades will see their arrangement work the other way around. The agreement is a first in English football.

BELIEVE IN THE SIGN

Wednesday players have proudly worn an owl on their jerseys for many years – since the early part of the twentieth century. A heraldic style coat of arms was used on stationery and programmes for a few years in the early 1950s though the notion of a crest was first introduced in 1956. It featured an Owl with the city's sheaves either side. Also included was Yorkshire's white rose and below these depictions the motto *Consilio et Animis*. Translated from Latin it means *By Wisdom and Courage*.

That changed in 1973 as a result of a competition among students at Granville College. 19-year-old Bob Walker scooped the prize and for almost two decades his simple Owl featured on virtually every official item, including the club's shirts. From 1985 the owl was perched on the initials *S.W.F.C.* and used throughout the next ten years until a return to something approaching the original design with an owl and branch. The club's initials were retained and placed either side of the bird. The county's rose became more prominent with a higher position and above all was the word Hillsborough. All of this was depicted within a shield. Slight tinkering continued until the Owl returned sat on the club's initials with the year of Wednesday's establishment below.

TAMING THE SHREWS

While Wednesday manager, the straight-talking Jack Charlton prepared his team for a meeting with Shrewsbury Town in February 1978. Discussing the day's opponents he went through various members of the Gay Meadow squad instructing Jeff Johnson to take care of fellow midfielder Brian Hornsby. His instructions were to watch out as the 'lad' was a skilful player. Charlton completed the talk by announcing 'I'm buying him to replace you.' Eighteen days later Johnson and Hornsby – who cost £45,000 – were team-mates and remained so for three years.

NINE OUT OF TEN SCORERS

Of the club's top ten marksmen, only nine have made it past a century of goals. Andrew Wilson is sole striker to have notched 200 or more.

Andrew Wilson	217
John Fantham	167
Redfern Froggatt	149
David Hirst	149
Ellis Rimmer	140
Mark Hooper	136
Fred Spiksley	114
Jimmy Trotter	114
David Mclean	100
Harry Chapman	99

Chapman is the sole man stuck on 99. On a purely games to goals ratio, Derek Dooley stands head and shoulders above all others. His 63 goals came from precisely 63 games and he became one of just five Wednesday players to finish as a divisional top scorer in 1951/52 by notching 46 in the league. David McLean is the only player to have achieved this twice over two concurrent seasons from 1911 to 1913. More impressively he did so in Division One. Jimmy Trotter managed to be the top flight's deadliest marksman in 1926/27 and is another prolific scorer from Wednesday's past with 114 from 160 appearances. Eddie Quigley scored 52 from his 78 games. David Layne has a similarly impressive record with 58 strikes from 81 outings.

HERE'S TO YOU, MR ROBINSON

Had it not been for the advent of the Second World War Jackie Robinson may well have gone on to claim one of the greatest league records of any Wednesday player – both as a goalscorer and possibly the number of games featured in. He started confidently enough with a debut goal just five days before the 1935 FA Cup final (his selection ensuring Ronnie Starling remained injury-free ahead of the Wembley date). However, Jackie couldn't keep a firm grip on his place for a couple of seasons. Plugging away in the reserves he proved his worth and was given an extended run during the 1936/37 term amassing 6 goals from 30 games. Not a terrific return on the face of it but he wasn't just in the side based on statistics; Robinson possessed attributes others could only marvel at. A naturally skilful player he produced deft body-swerves which took him away from covering defenders and bought space for colleagues which he ruthlessly exploited with telling passes. Sheer pace was another weapon in his armoury and one complimented by unerring control of the ball.

The last full season before battle raged against Hitler saw him score 19 times and although it wasn't quite enough to secure promotion for Wednesday. it whetted the appetite for the following term. The forward surpassed that form but with the professional game suspended it was outside first-class matches. Jackie made many appearances in the specially arranged regional competitions. From his 109 outings a staggering 91 goals were notched including six hat-tricks during the 1942/43 season alone when he scored at a rate of more than a goal a game. When the Football League resumed Robinson took his place in the side but was sold to Sunderland for £7,500 just 7 games and 6 goals into the 1946/47 campaign. The deal left many wondering what might have been had he stayed. However, his Tyneside birthplace plus continued residence in the area where he had also been stationed during the war meant training with Newcastle United and only reporting to Wednesday for games. This was deemed an inappropriate arrangement for any player, let alone the skipper. Injury ended his career five years later but a small revelation came during his switch to the North-East. It turned out that he was two years older than had been thought during his time at Wednesday.

THE ONE-UP CLUB

Despite hundreds, in some cases many hundreds, of appearances for Wednesday, some players have just one goal to show for all their efforts. Scoring certainly isn't the best way to gauge a player's contribution to the club but still makes very interesting reading. Among the most notable members of this select club is Don McEvoy who in 1955/56 captained the Owls to a Second Division championship. His only goal in 112 appearances came in a 4–2 defeat by Manchester City the season after top-flight status had been regained. Edgar Packard wasn't noted for his flair in the opposition's half either; so there were more than a few raised eyebrows when he scored a winner against West Ham United in December 1949. Not just by the fact he actually scored but that he took the ball from inside his own penalty area then rampaged upfield before a quick one-two with Clarrie Jordan set up that superb strike. At a rate of one goal every 181 games – including two appearances as a substitute – Sam Ellis is top of the tree for the most number of games to have yielded a single goal.

ABSOLUTELY SCORELESS

Full-back Ted Catlin failed to register in 230 first-team outings all made prior to the Second World War although he was on target during a 6–1 win over Notts County in 1944 – a North Regional Division game. Unfortunately he had no chance to double this return. The defender, who also turned out for Charlton Athletic during hostilities, was unable to resume his career in peacetime owing to his age and an injury sustained in the 1943 War Cup Final (North) against Blackpool which limited his effectiveness.

Hackney-born Des Walker was one of the finest defensive players of his age. Famously he only scored once in 857 games at club and international level; and that once was not in 361 outings for Sheffield Wednesday. His sole involvement in hitting the net came in his final season of his first spell at Nottingham Forest. On New Year's Day 1992, with Brian Clough's side trailing 1–0 to Luton Town, he made a rare bolt forward and managed to latch on to a pass down the middle. His surge was completed by lashing an effort past Steve Sutton, a keeper on loan from Forest. Walker's record doesn't improve when friendlies are factored in. Not so much as a penalty converted out of novelty value boosts his ratio. Indeed, such matches only push his career average beyond four figures.

QUICK OFF THE MARK

The scant nature of the early football record books makes giving the answer as to who has notched Wednesday's fastest goal a qualified one, but we can say that the fastest recorded goal scored by an Owls player came after 12 seconds when Charlie Tomlinson put the ball through Preston North End's net on 22 October 1949. It was the game's only goal and played at Deepdale. John Pearson was just a second behind when netting the opener in a 3–1 win over Bolton Wanderers in September 1982. That remains the quickest strike at Hillsborough.

WORTH HIS WEIGHT IN GOLD

Claiming a player is worth their weight in gold is an often-used phrase when handing out praise, but according to exchange rates in 1951 Jackie Sewell was valued as being exactly that when signed from Notts County at £34,500. Gold changed hands at $35 an ounce at the time which, when converted into sterling and physical weight, worked out to be just that amount.

TOP PRICES PAID

Paolo Di Canio's £4.7 million transfer from Celtic in August 1997 remains the club's highest sum ever shelled-out on a single player. Such a hefty amount and more straitened times means it may remain so. A decade later West Bromwich Albion were asked to part with £3 million to secure Chris Brunt. Although some payments depend on performances, the midfielder (who was picked up free from Middlesbrough) is set to meet if not exceed the conditions.

A quick analysis of Wednesday's transfer history shows just how quickly prices have spiralled. Clyde's Jimmy Blair was a big-money investment at £1,975 in 1914 and at the time set a club record which wasn't too far away from the highest amount exchanged between two British clubs. Tommy Craig attracted the first six-figure sum Wednesday paid in May 1969 and Peter Shirtliff's return to Hillsborough in 1989 cost the Owls their first £500,000-plus fee.

A HEAVY COST

Frank Westlake's signing from Thurnscoe Victoria in March 1938 proved costly in respect of the punishment meted out to Wednesday who failed to ensure his registration papers were in order ahead of a game at Luton Town. That administrative blunder meant the Owls had to do without his services for the remainder of their campaign. A heavy fine was also imposed and courtesy of war the full-back's next official outing came almost eight years after debut.

DEVASTATING DOOLEY

Despite spending just two full seasons in the Wednesday first team, Derek Dooley's standards remain the ones most Wednesday forwards are measured against. Former Owl Walter Millership watched the then teenage Lincoln City reserve smash a hat-trick against the Denaby United team he played for just after leaving Hillsborough. Scouting reports gave equally rave reviews. Dooley had been in devastating form for the Owls' second string but it took almost three years for him to make the senior ranks. Barnsley were the first team to feel his awesome talent for goalscoring at that level. In his third game, the unassuming striker scored both goals in a 2–1 win. By the close of the 1951/52 campaign he had bagged a record 47 league strikes including 5 in a single game against Notts County. Former Wednesday keeper Roy Smith was on duty for the Magpies. Also, 4 were recorded against Everton and Hull City. There were hat-tricks in wins over Brentford and West Ham United. A 9-game spell saw 22 strikes between late October and December 1951, those goals helping the Owls gain promotion to the First Division.

The higher grade of football seemed to overawe the striker at first and he was even dropped into the reserves. However, Dooley soon found himself back in the old routine and by the time Wednesday made the journey across the Pennines to Preston North End in February 1953, had scored a more than creditable 16 from 30 games. That brought his tally to 63 from as many outings, a ratio not just comparable with many of his peers but far better.

It was nothing short of a fairytale for the boy who once stood on the Kop but there was to be a cruel end to this promising career. Following a collision with Deepdale keeper George Thompson on an icy pitch, Dooley broke his leg. While such an injury wouldn't usually force a player into retirement the limb developed an infection and then gangrene set in, meaning it had to be removed in order to save his life. The problem – thought to be related to whitewash used to mark lines – was only discovered when the player asked one of the hospital staff who had been looking after him to sign his plaster cast. On brushing past the bed a nurse noticed there was no response from his foot which she would have expected to twitch. The player's condition worsened and all attempts to preserve the leg failed.

After taking a hand in coaching the youth team and an administrative job with Wednesday, Dooley returned to footballing side as manager in January 1971. However, replicating his on-field magic from the dugout proved tough. Attempts to regain the Owls' top-flight status never fared better than mid-table finishes although early during the 1972/73 season Wednesday were leading the division. Dooley was sacked on Christmas Eve 1973 after a run of poor results. In some respects these were prompted by a virus which swept through the club and remained a problem for a couple of months. This left little option but to try out anyone half fit and push players back before they were fully ready.

The results which came, unsurprisingly, left the side adrift at the foot of the table.

Despite taking a commercial role at Bramall Lane then serving as a director, managing director, chairman and vice-president of the Blades, Derek Dooley is fondly remembered by all who saw him play and his impact at Hillsborough was noted by the naming of a restaurant after him. His services to both Sheffield clubs and football elsewhere in the area saw him become an MBE. His death in 2008 was solemnly mourned by an entire city and further recognition came after his passing when a new section of ring road around Sheffield was named Derek Dooley Way.

DOING THEIR BIT FOR CHARITY

Wednesday have made two appearances in the Charity Shield, the traditional pre-season encounter between the reigning league champions and FA Cup holders. And both have seen Wednesday up against Arsenal. The first in 1930 as champions ended with a 2–1 defeat at Stamford Bridge. The second five years later was settled by a similarly narrow margin only this time in the Owls' favour courtesy of a Neil Dewar goal at Highbury.

HE PASSED THE AUDITION

John Ritchie was a popular figure at Stoke and with good reason – he averaged a goal every other game and ahead of his capture in the summer of 1966 bagged 30 from 47 outings. Wednesday secured his services, courtesy of a £70,000 bid which concluded a chase lasting 18 months, after the striker grabbed all 4 goals in a heavy defeat for the Owls. Wednesday lost over a quarter of their investment when the player returned to the Potteries three years later.

A LUCKY CHARM

Striker Jack Palethorpe didn't tend to stay long in one place but seemed to lead a charmed career. In his short spell with Stoke he lifted a Second Division title contributing 8 goals in 10 games after his transfer late in the 1932/33 season. Preston North End negotiated a deal early in the following campaign. At Deepdale he gained a second successive promotion to the top flight but a quick fade from the scene offered a chance with Wednesday. His £3,100 transfer proved money well spent and at Hillsborough he won the FA Cup. However, after losing his place the following term he joined Aston Villa and that luck ran out. There his contribution was limited and the Midlands outfit were relegated at the end of the season.

THE IMPORTANCE OF BEING ERNEST

For as long as Sheffield Wednesday exist it is unlikely the club will have had a better left-back than Ernie Blenkinsop. Not only the Owls' first choice he was also the finest player

England had in that position. The £1,000 which brought him to Hillsborough from Hull City may seem pretty small beer in the current climate but in January 1923 it was a sizeable fee. Speaking of beer, £100 plus 80 pints of ale for team-mates at his amateur club in Cudworth was the first transfer fee this former coal miner attracted.

Hull's loss was certainly Wednesday's gain as 424 games plus two league championships over the 12 years in which he captained both club and country demonstrate. The 26 caps earned made him Wednesday's most decorated England international until Ron Springett broke the record in the 1960s. Vision, control and passing were particular virtues of his game not widely exercised by a number of defensive contemporaries and even if some could match a few of his abilities, they would struggle to have earned the same high level of plaudits. A cool-headed presence at the back, he played an integral part in steering the Owls from a very average Second Division outfit into back-to-back championship-winners from 1928 to 1930. In March 1934 he transferred to Liverpool then joined Cardiff City ahead of the Second World War – an event which effectively ended his career. Though a participant in war games with Yorkshire sides once the conflict ended, he became a publican. Sheffield and other cities mourned his death in 1969.

LICENSED TO PLAY

Tom Brandon was offered ownership of a pub in return for defecting from Blackburn Rovers ahead of the Owls' maiden season in the Football League. He duly accepted becoming one the first players to sell beer *while* playing rather than *after* retiring. The defender failed to gain selection for Rovers' victory over Wednesday in the 1890 FA Cup final.

TERMS & CONDITIONS APPLY

The high value of professional players leads many to have clauses inserted in their contracts prohibiting all manner of activities from the clearly dangerous to the seemingly mundane. Former Owls' defender Tony Crane breached his contract with Boston United by playing as a keeper on the Sheffield Sunday League scene. There was also dissatisfaction with his attitude to training and serious concerns over his weight. The man sometimes utilised as striking cover during his time at Hillsborough later had a stint with Hallam FC.

Long before turning up at Hillsborough, Chris Waddle, who played Sunday League football with The Devonshire Arms and Brushmeer Athletic after hanging up his boots, was rumoured to have an agreement in his Newcastle United contract ensuring he would not play against his boyhood favourites Sunderland. Talk started after he missed the few Tyne & Wear derbies during his stint at St James' Park. However, on each occasion the winger had been injured. After catching the eye in amateur football Waddle had a fortnight's trial at Roker Park. This used all his leave entitlement at the sausage-seasoning factory he earned a living from, and meant he couldn't take up a similar offer from Newcastle made just days after Sunderland ended their interest. Fortunately the Magpies remained keen and signed him a few months later.

WEDNESDAY IN EUROPE

Wednesday have made three journeys into Europe, the first being their most successful. Finishing as runners-up at the close of the 1960/61 campaign saw the Owls invited to play in a competition then known as the Inter-City Fairs Cup. French side Lyon provided the first hurdle and Wednesday returned from the opening leg trailing 4–2. However, a 5–2 win at Hillsborough calmed nerves and earned a 7–6 aggregate win. AS Roma were dispatched more easily and a 4–0 win in the first match – with Gerry Young grabbing a hat-trick – could not be overturned a fortnight later in Italy. The quarter-final draw paired the Owls with the mighty Barcelona. The Spanish giants were edged out in the first game 3–2 but made home advantage count at the Nou Camp with a 2–0 victory on the night, giving them a 4–3 aggregate win.

A sixth-place finish earned another shot at the continent two years later. The going was a little tougher for the 1963/64 campaign and ended at the hands of crack West German side FC Cologne in the second phase. Despite a laudable 3–2 away victory, Wednesday saw their good work come to nothing after a 2–1 reverse at Hillsborough. DOS Utrecht had been easily disposed of in the opening round. The Owls should have been given a go the previous year but the FA decided it had the right to choose which clubs would go forward to face continental opposition. They opted to share entry around the league rather than use final league standings as a guide. To rub further salt in the wound, Sheffield United were initially proposed. However, in the end only Everton were given the chance. The FA were arbiters of the game in England so the Fairs Cup committee, who had initially invited Wednesday to participate, accepted that nomination. Appeals were not allowed.

The Owls went out at the same stage in 1992/93 when the club's best finish since the 1960s gave them another opportunity to take on Europe's best. Twenty years earlier the continent's governing body had assumed control of the competition and their rebranded UEFA Cup, with entrance based purely on merit, held an enormous amount of esteem. Many believed there was a real chance of progression to the latter stages, especially as CA Spora Luxembourg were hammered 10–2 in the first round. However, a tough assignment against FC Kaiserslautern put paid to all ambitions. A 3–1 away defeat then the sharing of 4 goals at Hillsborough saw the Germans through 5–3 on aggregate.

A place in Europe would have been achieved six years earlier but for the ban imposed on English clubs after the Heysel Stadium Disaster. Wednesday finished fifth at the close of the 1985/86 campaign. There was also disappointment during the summer of 2000 when the Owls missed out on a UEFA Cup place thanks to a lottery. Due to the club's good disciplinary record the previous season, Wednesday were entered into a draw with 11 other sides. The first two names out of the hat – Belgian and Spanish clubs as it turned out – received the prize. Wednesday's only consolation was a £5,000 cheque for their efforts

A TOTO WASTE OF TIME?

Faced with the apparent threat of having their clubs banned from European competition the Premier League felt compelled to enter three teams into the 1995 Intertoto Cup. Places in the UEFA Cup had been made available to each of the four semi-finalists – which peaked interest until it was realised that the competition started in late June. Consequently training would need to start just weeks after the previous season ended. Sheffield Wednesday joined Tottenham Hotspur and Wimbledon as participants. Each treated the competition with less than complete enthusiasm but the London clubs received a year-long embargo on participation for the level of contempt shown.

The Owls utilised many players from their youth ranks. In their first game with Basel only two recognised first-teamers – Graham Hyde and Michael Williams – were included in the travelling party but Wednesday were at virtual full strength for the concluding three group games. Finishing second in their section to Karlsruher SC ended participation at the earliest possible stage. Only getting through another two rounds squeezed into a few days or so would have earned what was now viewed as the less than coveted reward.

A handful of players turned out for Wednesday in this competition only and no other first-team games. These include five of six temporary signings made for the opener. Former Owl John Pearson, a veteran of more than 100 games in his time at Hillsborough, was drafted in from Cardiff City for a nice swansong, while Andy Williams and Tony O'Brien came in from Rotherham United. The others to make just one loan outing are Ian Bowling of Bradford City and Halifax Town's David German. Of those on the permanent staff, Richard Barker and Peter Holmes only have their participation in this tournament to look back on as Wednesday men.

Home games were played at Millmoor rather than Hillsborough which does mean that the escapade created a good quiz question – when did Rotherham United host European football?

THE NIGHT PETER SPRINGETT HELD THE EUROPEAN CUP

A host of Wednesday players have lifted the European Cup, unfortunately all at clubs they joined either before or after turning up at Hillsborough. One managed to do so when the famous silverware had been stolen. With future Owls Pat Heard and Andy Blair in their number, Aston Villa won the trophy in 1982 and as so often was the case, victorious players took the enormous trophy to a local pub. Colin Gibson allowed locals at a Tamworth hostelry a close look only for a light-fingered tippler to simply smuggle it away. While panic reigned in the Midlands, the trophy – still resplendent in claret and blue ribbons – was handed in at the front desk of Sheffield's West Bar police station in the wee small hours. On duty that night was a retired Peter Springett who appeared in snaps taken by bobbies as a memento of their shift. Officers not only held the cup, they staged an impromptu four-a-side game for the prize before ensuring a return to the holders. Peter later became a Community Constable at Sheffield United.

THE CHEMICAL BROTHERS

David Weatherall combined attempts to make his way through Wednesday's junior ranks with gaining a Chemistry degree from the University of Sheffield. Between lectures and probably various experiments requiring goggles, the boyhood Owl would turn out for the reserves before a move to Leeds United ahead of his finals. In 1991 his home city hosted the World Student Games. The centre-half was part of Great Britain's bronze medal-winning squad. At the other end of his career, Barry Horne pitched up at Hillsborough almost seventeen years after gaining first class honours in the same subject from the University of Liverpool. Unlike Weatherall, who has remained in the game as a coach, the former Welsh international returned to education combining the teaching of chemistry and physics with a director of football role at a Chester school.

HEAVY LOSS

Although not a subject too many Owls like to dwell on, there have been occasions when Wednesday sides have been completely outclassed and suffered thrashings as a result. The worst of these defeats came at the hands of Aston Villa who recorded their 10–0 win in a First Division game on 5 October 1912. Fortunately the match was played at Villa Park – a real bogey ground at the time – at least sparing the Hillsborough faithful humiliation on their own territory.

Nottingham Forest ensured the home fans left the stadium with their tails between their legs late in the 1994/95 season. Only one reply could be mustered against the seven Wednesday conceded for their record home defeat. Appropriately the game was played on April Fools' Day.

The club's worst defeats in domestic cup competitions are:

FA Cup   Blackburn Rovers   1–6   29 March 1890
League Cup   Queens Park Rangers   2–8   6 November 1973

OLDEST ...

It isn't easy to ascertain the birth dates of some players from Wednesday's early years but where information is verifiable it can be said that then manager Trevor Francis made his final appearance for the club on 20 November 1993 aged 39 years and 215 days. Andrew Wilson is the next most senior player to have played for the Owls back on 10 March 1920 – 91 days past his 39th birthday.

Jeremiah Jackson, 46 years old, had had nothing more than training exercises under his belt for many seasons when he was an emergency addition to the team due to play at Port Vale in August 1923. Two players failed to show so the Owls' coach turned out on the right wing. Some said he had to leave the field after 15 minutes but most reports suggest he lasted more than half an hour.

Although some record books say Tom Brittleton was the oldest player to have made a first-team appearance for

Wednesday, the half-back was 38 years and 8 days old at the point of his last game for the Owls on 1 May 1920. That Brittleton became the oldest Wednesday player to turn out in a Football League game at the time is no surprise given the outstanding level of fitness exhibited during his 15 years with the club. Great strength was a contributing factor to this and though a stern tackler, Brittleton always seemed to get up totally unscathed. Even after the former captain left Wednesday he played another five seasons of top-grade football by joining Stoke and was still viewed as an integral member of the side prior to his leaving for hometown club Winsford United where he combined playing with management duties.

Eric Nixon was on the coaching staff during the 2003/04 season. Just a week before his 41st birthday the veteran keeper, only hired on a part-time basis, helped breach an injury crisis when Ola Tidman and Chris Stringer were ruled out. He had only expected to be on the bench but found himself brought on when Kevin Pressman had to be withdrawn just 28 minutes into a league game with Grimsby Town during September. Hillsborough was the final stop in a career spanning more than two decades, 13 clubs (some with more than one spell) and almost 1,100 games.

YOUTH CUP

The Owls' youth side reached the FA Youth Cup final for the first, and to date only, time in 1991 coming up against Millwall. The Lions took the tie 3–0 on aggregate. All the goals came in a terrible first leg at Hillsborough.

WE'RE HERE EVERY WEEK

Don Megson and Martin Hodge are the club's most consistent appearance-makers in terms of ever-present seasons. Both mustered four fully completed campaigns during their lengthy Hillsborough careers.

WHO'S THE YOUNGEST?

Making his debut at 15 years and 269 days, Peter Fox became – and remains – the youngest ever Owl to make a senior outing. With Peter Grummitt and Peter Springett out, the keeper faced Leyton Orient on 31 March 1973, maintaining a clean sheet in a 2–0 win. That broke Gary Scothorn's mark of 16 years and 257 days set on 18 February 1967. Further chances took time and Fox led an intriguing career which included a summer loan at Team Hawaii in the North American Soccer League during 1977. An opportunity to join Stoke City was one the Scunthorpe-born stopper would never regret as it allowed him to play in Division One and though the Staffordshire side couldn't retain their place among the elite, he made well over 400 outings in the Potteries before retirement called at the ripe old age of 42 while a player/coach at Exeter City.

Necessity will see managers blood youngsters and at 16 years and 205 days old Matthew Bowman was called into Paul Sturrock's plans as a result of a chronic injury crisis early in the 2006/07 season. A chance came with 15 minutes remaining against Wrexham in the Carling Cup. Though the game ended in a shock 4–1 home reverse and Bowman gained no further opportunities – leaving Hillsborough when that campaign ended – those bare statistics make the striker Wednesday's youngest ever outfield player. Mark Platts' previous record was shaved by 58 days.

FESTIVE FIXTURES & FRUSTRATIONS

These days players are allowed to spend a large part of Christmas Day with their families. With such a busy festive period it is seen as the right thing to do. However, it wasn't always so. Until 1958 and with very few exceptions players up and down the country would be expected to turn out on 25 December. Wednesday's last fixture on this date was in 1957 when Hillsborough witnessed a thrilling 4–4 draw with Preston North End. A player who never featured in any of these matches was Jack Earp. A very religious man, Earp would not play on Christmas Day. But for his faith the full-back would have added to the 174 appearances made before leaving in 1900. In tandem with Ambrose Langley, he built one of the best partnerships in the Football League.

On the subject of Christmas/New Year fixtures, until 1995 the Owls hadn't won all of their festive games for 85 years.

A TESTIMONY TO LONG SERVICE

Testimonial years are the traditional reward for players who have put in at least 10 years' service with a club. Almost 40 players have spent a decade or more at Hillsborough if you count those with one or more spells. This figure is whittled down a little further when only those who spent a continuous period at Hillsborough are taken into account. Andrew Wilson weighs in as the longest-server at 19 years 192 days. This figure is based on his debut made on 1 September 1900 and his last game for the club on 10 March 1920. Redfern Froggatt also spent the best part of two decades at the club although the first three years were during the latter part of the Second World War.

Off the field Eric Taylor had 45 years of service in various capacities. Starting as an office boy under manager Bobby Brown he rose to general manager by retirement in 1974. Taylor was first-team boss from 1942 to 1958 during which time he won two Second Division championships and guided the side to another top-flight promotion via the runners-up spot in 1950. He had a keen eye for good players and how he could fit them into the side. He bought Jackie Sewell for a club record £35,000. He also signed keeper Peter Springett who would blossom into a regular England international and introduced the young talents of Derek Dooley, Albert Quixall and John Fantham. Relegation in 1958 during what became known as the yo-yo years persuaded him that change was required in order for the club to progress.

THOSE WHO ALSO SERVE

Another Eric, Eric England, also began life at Hillsborough as an office boy but served higher offices with distinction especially in his last post of general-secretary. A far less celebrated but no less distinguished figure at Hillsborough was Harry Liversidge. Although he officially served as caretaker from 1930 until his day of retirement aged 76 in 1965, he was the club's only employee throughout the Second World War and undertook a host of duties, including that of first-team trainer. For approximately four decades (indeed, until the same year Liversidge called it a day) Vin Hardy, Billy Betts's brother-in-law, kept things neat and tidy on the Kop end. Throughout all its developments from a simple bank of ashes and cinder, Vin remained making sure the area was clean and rubbish-free before and after games. He celebrated his 80th birthday in that post. At one stage his horse also pulled the manual grass-cutter and roller around the pitch.

A CAREER IN SHORT MEASURE

At the other end of the scale is David Armstrong, a driving midfielder who joined Wednesday in the summer of 1987 after six seasons with Southampton and a lengthy spell with Middlesbrough. Howard Wilkinson saw the 33-year-old's recruitment as a way of injecting much-needed experience into his squad. However, matters away from the field led Armstrong to redress his situation within hours of the ink drying on his freshly penned contract. Whisked away to join a pre-season tour of West Germany a day after being signed, introductions were still being made to new colleagues just ahead of a meeting with Arminia Bielefeld. Armstrong played but asked for a meeting with his new boss soon after the final whistle. The pair talked for some hours and agreed that a club nearer to his former employers would be found. The split was amicable and a transfer to AFC Bournemouth arranged. Unfortunately, a serious injury ended his career not long after. Armstrong later explained that his son's college course was not one he could pursue in Sheffield which meant either he had to live separate from his family or his teenage son would have to remain alone on the south coast.

PATIENCE WAS KEY

Lance Key gained 47 minutes as Kevin Pressman's replacement between the posts against Gillingham during a third round FA Cup game in January 1995. A £10,000 buy from Histon, this was Key's big chance but his first touch was to pick the ball out of the net. A replacement keeper was needed due to Pressman's dismissal in giving away a penalty just before the break. Wednesday led 2–0 at the time and though the spot-kick went in, Key – who had spent almost six years at Hillsborough – was possibly the man who did most to ensure the Owls held on for victory and didn't fall to the Third Division outfit. However, that was to be his only opportunity as Chris Woods had fought back from injury by the time Pressman's suspension kicked in. Over the summer Key joined Dundee United.

DERBY DAYS

The Steel City derby remains one of the most fiercely contested rivalries in European football. Strictly speaking it is the oldest too, although the earliest competitive encounter between clubs from the city wasn't a United and Wednesday clash. It was an FA Cup tie between Sheffield FC and Sheffield Providence in 1879 – the Blades and Owls only met 11 years later. From the 125 games played since both teams entered the Football League, Sheffield United hold the whip hand with 4 more victories than Wednesday have recorded – 45 to 41, with 39 games drawn.

The two clubs pitted their wits against each other for the first time on 15 December 1890 in a friendly. Despite the match being played on a Monday afternoon just before Christmas, 10,000 fans ventured out to the Olive Grove. Overhead the sky was as grey as Wednesday's recent form. The hosts were bottom of the Football Alliance and went behind after 20 minutes. However, there was absolutely no question of Wednesday letting their upstart neighbours ease to a win, especially not on home territory. Toddles Woolhouse's persistence paid off when he equalised early in the second half. It looked like honours would finish even but with time short in supply Wednesday continued plugging away and with five minutes left Harry Winterbottom notched the deciding goal. The Bramall Lane return a few weeks later proved just as pulsating. This time it was Wednesday's turn to draw first blood and when the advantage was stretched it seemed an otherwise damp squib of a season would be brightened by claiming an historic double. However, United rallied claiming a 3–2 victory.

The initial meeting between the two clubs in the Football League took place after the Blades' elevation to Division One on Monday 16 October 1893 at Bramall Lane and finished all square. The first at Hillsborough ended in disappointment as Sheffield United edged it 2–1. Wednesday didn't taste league victory over United until September 1895 when Lawrence Bell's goal separated the sides. There was no win at Bramall Lane for seven seasons when another tight game finished 3–2. The Owls' worst defeat came on 8 September 1951 courtesy of a 7–3 reverse.

Wednesday have the best unbeaten run in the fixture – 11 matches from October 1910 to October 1919.

Wednesday's best victory came when both teams were at a low ebb in Division Three. The Owls recorded a 4–0 home win on Boxing Day 1979 in a match referred to as the 'Boxing Day Massacre'. In League One during the 2011/12 season the bitter rivals would again be up against each other.

BATTING ABOVE THEIR AVERAGE

By far the most intriguing set of derby games took place at the end of the 1930s when United and Wednesday players clashed in a series of cricket matches at Bramall Lane. Given both club's historical roots it seems a rather fitting challenge.

HOME NATIONS

Nigel Worthington is the most capped Wednesday player and 50 of his 66 appearances for Northern Ireland came during his time at Hillsborough. Ron Springett was awarded more England caps than any other with 33 international appearances while an Owl. From the other home nations Andrew Wilson holds the most Scotland caps with 6. Welsh midfielder Mark Pembridge earned 18 call-ups while at Hillsborough and the Republic of Ireland's John Sheridan was awarded 27 caps during his time in S6.

Charles Clegg played in the first international game to be held anywhere in the world as part of the travelling England team which met Scotland in Glasgow. Given the notoriety of the occasion he couldn't do anything but become the first Wednesday player to be awarded an international cap as the game finished 0–0. Ernest Blenkinsop skippered England for the first time against Spain in December 1931. He led the team on 4 further occasions only ending up on the losing side once when earning his 26th and last cap – a 2–1 defeat to Scotland at Hampden Park. The left-back created a record at the time as all his international honours came in consecutive matches between May 1928 and April 1933.

NATIONAL COACHES

Nigel Worthington and Dave Clements are Owls who have managed the Northern Ireland national side – the latter's 11th and final game in charge was also his last cap. There are other Wednesday players to have taken control of a country's footballing ambitions. For the home nations Howard Wilkinson had two one-game stints in caretaker charge of England after Glenn Hoddle and Kevin Keegan left their posts in 1999 and 2000 respectively. Not long after finishing his spell as Hillsborough boss, Jack Charlton earned acclaim as Republic of Ireland boss guiding the country to World Cup and European Nations Cup finals.

Outside the British Isles Dave Russell coached Denmark just after the Second World War ended while Fred Spiksley was named Sweden boss in 1911, although opposition from Gothenberg delegates ensured that post was only held in the short term. Fred had hoped to guide the Scandanavians at the Olympics they were due to host a year later but when the reluctant faction altered their position ahead of that tournament, he declined their offer. Jack Reynolds was briefly in charge of the Netherlands after the First World War.

The well-travelled Ian Porterfield took charge of Zambia who he rebuilt after their entire squad perished in a plane crash and came within one goal of World Cup qualification – all in a matter of months. Posts with Zimbabwe, Oman plus Trinidad and Tobago followed. At the time of his death in 2007 he was Armenia's national coach. Colin Dobson led Bahrain in the 1980s while Mick Lyons took charge of Brunei on two occasions. Mike Hennigan held interim charge of Malawi and Mark Chamberlain had the furthest-flung role becoming an assistant-coach with East Timor – one of world football's weakest teams at the time. His stay in South-East Asia lasted just four months as an offer to join Portsmouth's backroom team was snapped up.

FROM FOREIGN SOIL

Albeit less than a roaring success, Yugoslavian Ante Mirocevic's signing from FK Budućnost in 1980 made him the first foreign player to sign for the Owls. He has been followed by more than 50 others representing all corners of the globe.

INTERNATIONAL FOLLY

Parisian Yoann Folly was a French youth international signed by Paul Sturrock from old club Southampton in order to overcome an injury crisis. The temporary transfer was made permanent but a lack of opportunity saw the midfielder look for a change of surroundings less than two years later. By that time Folly was a potential Togo international having transferred allegiance to the African nation through family heritage. Despite being named in Togo's 2006 World Cup squad he withdrew as a response to positive noises from France. Those soundings failed to yield anything above the under-21 caps already secured so Folly performed a u-turn eventually representing his adopted nation in August 2008 while a Plymouth Argyle player. Sturrock had moved on to Home Park in the intervening time and linked up with his charge for a third and, to date, final time.

OUCH!

In just his second game for Wednesday Laurie Bell was thrown into the cauldron of a Sheffield derby and came up against the Blades' man mountain of a keeper, William Foulke, for the first time. United's custodian was an imposing figure standing higher than 6ft tall and weighing in excess of 20 stones. Perhaps Bell thought that made the United man second favourite for a cross but Foulke made full use of his height advantage, took the catch and fell to earth. A softer landing than expected came as the striker was sandwiched between his ample frame and the turf. That huge amount of weight and both knees crashing into Bell's back could have caused serious damage. Foulke actually believed he may have killed him but after some treatment the forward was able to carry on. From that point he often thought twice about some aerial confrontations although did manage to score the game's only goal.

HEALTH & SAFETY

After a long battle to establish himself as Peter Shilton's successor in England's national side once the 1990 World Cup ended, Chris Woods handed a chance to another up-and-coming deputy David Seaman just six weeks before the tournament. Attempting to release a troublesome drawstring waistband on his tracksuit bottoms with a penknife Woods cut a finger and couldn't take his place on the bench against Czechoslovakia. The slip didn't prove too costly in the short term. Woods was back for the next international and retained as first choice between the sticks until the summer of 1993 when Seaman's claims could no longer be denied.

Marcus Tudgay added his name to the list of footballers to suffer strange injuries when he missed the 2006/07 season's first month. During a summer barbecue he stepped on a glass bottle which then shattered severing tendons in a toe which needed surgery to repair. An initial prognosis that he could be out for a period approaching four months proved wrong and full rehabilitation took ten weeks.

NICE WORK IF YOU CAN GET IT

Scottish international James J. Lang, or 'Reddie' as he was commonly known, topped-up his income handsomely from football. Those bountiful supplements came under threat when he lost an eye as a result of an accident at his day job, working in a Clyde shipyard. It was something he kept secret so as not to give opponents an edge. When Glasgow's association played their Sheffield counterparts in 1876 he came to the attention of Wednesday. Though purporting to be an amateur Lang was anything but having employment yet no duties at a company owned by a Wednesday board member – one which manufactured metal knives and cutting implements.

Within a year Reddie returned to Scotland turning out for former clubs Clydesdale and Third Lanark. With the latter he played in a Scottish Cup final. International honours were also won before a second spell with Wednesday. This time his stay lasted far longer but while surreptitious payments had their advantages, Lang and others could still have their heads turned. The vehemently professional Burnley didn't require their players to have bogus jobs and led a breakaway football association which gave birth to an age of openly paid professionals. This proved too big a temptation for Lang to resist. Clarets' players could earn as much as £2 per week – almost double what many other clubs would offer their international players and four times as much as most others could hope to earn.

COMEBACKS

One of the most remarkable comebacks on record was achieved by The Wednesday in a Division One game with Everton at Owlerton on 12 November 1904. Trailing 5–1 at the break an excellent rally saw the Owls claw a way back and reduce the gap to a single goal as the final seconds approached. Matters were helped when visiting keeper Billy Scott was forced off with the score at 5–3. His duties were undertaken by left-half Walter Abbott although Harry Davis's dismissal ensured the numbers stayed the same for most of the second period. Keen to ensure the pressure they faced was limited, the ball was smashed high into the Wednesday fans by a visiting player incurring the officials' wrath and a minute's added time. In that brief window Bob Ferrier managed to put another past Abbott tying the scores at 5–5.

The club's earliest return from a seemingly lost position came in the final of the first Sheffield Challenge Cup in March 1877. In those pre-Sheffield United days Heeley FC provided Wednesday's arch rivals. Heeley held a 3–0 half-time lead but a fightback began with Tom and Frank Butler's goals. Not long before the game's end William Clegg notched an equaliser sending the game into extra time. With the wind very much in their sails Wednesday found themselves in the ascendancy. Of the chances created, Bill Skinner made sure his counted thereby writing himself into club folklore by scoring the winner and completing a most unlikely victory.

As reigning European champions Manchester United would have seemed good value for a win before a match with Wednesday on 31 August 1968 kicked off. After all, while United had claimed the ultimate prize on offer to European clubs, Wednesday had narrowly averted relegation. The Owls' fortunes had picked up after just one defeat in the season's opening six games but they remained overwhelming underdogs. When Jack Whitham gained an advantage two minutes in, the majority of the crowd were merely hoping that the hosts could retain it but with half time looming United turned the game on its head building a 4–2 lead. With all their leading stars on show and shining, the game looked over as a contest. However, Whitham notched his second moments before the break. Unbelievably an equaliser came just after the restart when David Ford's free-kick was deflected by Nobby Stiles' head. Whitham's proximity to the World Cup winner led some to believe he had got the final touch. If his claims to that goal were in question there were no doubts when he netted from close range 20 minutes from the final whistle. This time Wednesday held on to seal a remarkable win.

FEET OF CLAY

According to the country's National Museum the entire Republic of Ireland team that beat England in the 1988 European Championship finals – Wednesday's John Sheridan included – had Gartan clay in their boots. A piece of earth from the town in County Donegal is said to be carried by many Irish families as it protects from fire, vermin and death. All without any need for a priest.

UNBEATEN & UNWINNABLE RUNS

Wednesday's finest start to a season came in the first season at Owlerton. A 14-match unbeaten run began the 1899/1900 campaign. Twelve matches were won in that streak which Chesterfield ended at Saltergate with a tight 1–0 victory. The Spirites also brought Wednesday's worst start to a campaign to a halt as the 1977/78 season saw Wednesday take 11 games to register a win (5 games were drawn and 6 lost). Former Liverpool reserve striker Tommy Tynan ended the sequence by scoring the only goal in a win over Chesterfield.

The Owls' best sequence without a defeat was the 19 league games won or drawn during the 1960/61 season. A 5–4 win over Blackburn Rovers just over a fortnight before Christmas began the run of form which took in six draws among the victories enjoyed. That narrow win over Blackburn was also an indication of the high-scoring encounters to come until Spurs won 2–1 at White Hart Lane in the middle of April. On the road Fulham were beaten 6–1 while Preston were sent back across the Pennines on the back of a 5–1 hammering. Also during this period only one cup game was lost, Burnley knocking the Owls off the road to Wembley in the sixth round after a replay at Turf Moor. Frustratingly Wednesday had secured victory by the odd goal in seven just under a month earlier at the same venue.

THE FATHER OF TOTAL FOOTBALL

Manchester-born Jack Reynolds may best be described as an ordinary winger in his less than celebrated playing days. His better times came outside the Football League, especially with New Brompton – later to become Gillingham. He made just a couple of outings for Wednesday debuting in a 3–3 home draw with Sunderland during April 1906, then waiting in the reserves for 51 weeks until given a second and final opportunity when Wednesday entertained Stoke. A release when the season ended allowed for that move to Kent.

Something of an innovator tactically, Reynolds could find little opportunity to enter coaching in England but impressed Swiss outfit FC St Gallen who offered him their manager's post. Just ahead of the First World War his exploits earned the chance to be named the first ever coach of Germany's national team. However, with battle set to rage across Europe – his homeland and prospective employers on opposite sides – he resiled from the contract. That perhaps proved serendipitous as Ajax from the Dutch capital, Amsterdam, were keen to step in and offer a chance to succeed Jack Kirwan who was returning to Ireland. The Dutch valued British and Irish coaches highly and the Netherlands' neutrality provided an opportunity to work unfettered. Over three stints at the helm Reynolds not only won the club's debut national title – the first of eight under his stewardship – he secured a cup win. Most importantly he founded the youth system which has mined a host of world-class talents and continues to function well almost a century on.

Added to this is the principle of Total Football, a fluid but organised structure which allows the maintenance of team shape and easy adaptation to attacking or defending, which Reynolds decreed would be practised from the senior team down to the most junior ranks. This made players comfortable at turning out in a number of positions rather than just accept that physical attributes made them more suitable to certain roles. With some modifications and tweaks this took Ajax to their peak in the 1970s with three successive European Cups. The system also brought Holland to the brink of becoming World Cup winners on more than one occasion. Reynolds made the Netherlands his home – a decision which saw him interned in a prisoner of war camp by the Nazis – but didn't live to see the end product of his work, passing away in 1962. That was a dozen years before Rinus Michels – a man he mentored as both a player and coach – almost claimed international football's biggest prize. Reynolds took charge of the Dutch national side for a single game in 1919. A stand at Ajax's then home ground, the De Meer Stadion, was named in his honour.

SHARING THE SPOILS

The club record for most draws recorded in a single season is 19 during the 1978/79 Third Division campaign.

THE MAN WHO TURNED DOWN ANGELINA JOLIE

Wayne Andrews, who spent a successful six weeks on loan from Coventry City in the later months of 2006, was one of the footballers employed to appear in *Mean Machine* with Vinnie Jones five years before his temporary switch to

Hillsborough. However, acting failed to lure the striker away from a football career. Not long after that silver screen debut, the winger turned down a part in *Lara Croft Tomb Raider: The Cradle of Life* and the chance to appear alongside Angelina Jolie. He had been offered a contract with Oldham Athletic and decided the distraction wasn't needed if he was to make a success of that move. When asked about his favourite film Andrews names *The Shawshank Redemption* as his choice.

Also at the movies, John Harkes portrayed one of the USA internationals to have caused the shock defeat of England in the 1950 World Cup entitled *The Game of Their Lives*. Intriguingly the man from New Jersey was asked to adopt a Scottish accent as he played Greenock-born emigrant skipper Ed McIlvenny. However, in the film McIlvenny, who joined Manchester United soon after the tournament, was not depicted as the captain. His role and influence were also scaled down, one of Hollywood's many historical liberties. Harkes is a celebrated commentator on US networks but less well regarded as a thespian. His only other role, unaccredited, was a brief part in a 2007 edition of *Without a Trace*.

Marc Degryse and Orlando Trustfull had parts in *The Full Monty* but found themselves on the cutting room floor.

OWN GOALS

Wednesday may not have been credited with the fastest own goal in British football but have come as close as any other club to troubling the current mark. Yet the 13 seconds it took Steve Bould to woefully miscue an attempt to play safe and pass the ball back to John Lukic at Hillsborough in February 1990 is still more than twice the current record.

Few incidents in football are truly unique but as far as anyone can say Sheffield Wednesday are the only team to have recorded a goal without a single player from the scoring side touching the ball. When attempting to discharge early danger, Fulham and England's Alan Mullery put through his own net 30 seconds after kick-off in a match played on 21 January 1961. It was a bad day for the Cottagers who eventually lost the game 6–1. Wednesday were in generous spirit themselves against West Bromwich Albion on Boxing Day 1952 the Baggies ran out 5–4 winners in no small part thanks to Norman Curtis and Eddie Gannon putting the ball past their own keeper.

THE BEAUTIFUL GAMES

Wednesday have played a range of clubs in friendlies. Santos, the Brazilian side who boasted the talents of Pelé until his twilight years were spent in the North American Soccer League, are possibly the most famous and have visited Hillsborough twice. Arguably the greatest player to ever grace a football field turned out in both. For the first held in 1962 many of the visiting players were part of the reigning World Cup-winning squad and ran out comfortable 4–2 victors. An eager 49,058 fans watched a piece of history when Pelé – twice a world champion at the tender age of 21 – placed the ball on the spot after a foul had been punished. As one the crowd held its breath. Ron Springett probably took a few deep ones too as the opportunity was dispatched with ease. The keeper simply didn't move but it was virtually Pelé's only chance. Peter Swan was outstanding keeping the shackles on throughout 90 minutes.

Ten years later Santos and Pelé returned. Although an afternoon kick-off due to the ongoing miners' strike, Sheffield was buzzing and a crowd in excess of 45,000 were on hand to witness a 2–0 Santos win – one of the goals came when Peter Grummitt slammed a goalkick against one of the Brazilian players which ricocheted in.

WORLD CUP OWLS

Just six players have been selected for World Cup duty while on Sheffield Wednesday's books. The first was Albert Quixall who at 20 years of age was the youngest member of England's squad for the 1954 finals in Switzerland. The striker didn't play and eight years later Peter Swan went to Chile but wasn't selected for duty. Consequently Ron Springett was the first Wednesday man to feature in a game during the finals. He played in each of England's four games during that 1962 tournament. By the time England played host four years later the keeper had been usurped by Gordon Banks and looked on as his nation were crowned champions. Almost three and half decades on, Springett and others who only acted as reserves received the winner's medals denied to them by strict FIFA regulations.

The full list is as follows:

Albert Quixall	England	1954
Ron Springett	England	1962 and 1966
Peter Swan	England	1962
Nigel Worthington	Northern Ireland	1986
John Sheridan	Republic of Ireland	1990 and 1994
Roland Nilsson	Sweden	1994

OLIVER PRIZE

Just under six months after their formation, Wednesday won the Cromwell Cup on the first and only time it was contested, beating the Garrick Club 1–0 in extra time on 15 February 1868 at Bramall Lane. The trophy had been devised for clubs less than two years old by the manager of the Theatre Royal, Oliver Cromwell (though clearly not the one who did for King Charles I), who also played for the Garrick. The silverware remains on display in the club's trophy room and this was the first game and cup ever to be decided by a golden goal. It took ten minutes of indefinite extra time after the final whistle sounding for The Wednesday to net.

THE LONG ...

The tallest player ever to represent Sheffield Wednesday is a remarkable man, not for his playing record, which was modest, but his sheer size in an era when the average height was little more than a metre and a half (in Edwardian times those who stood over 6ft tall were considered relative giants). The 6ft 6in Percy Kite had made ad hoc appearances for Manchester City and other clubs in his native north-west during the war years but was no more than someone aspiring to gain a professional contract when the First World War ceased. Sheffield Wednesday were one of the clubs he had an audition with though unusually he gained that chance in first team – the 1919/20 season's final game and a 1–0 win over Oldham Athletic. It was his only outing before moving on.

... AND THE SHORT OF IT

Teddy Davison the smallest keeper to play for England and Wednesday stood just 5ft 7in tall in his stocking feet but was as agile as a cat, brave as a lion and anticipated a forward's next move extremely well. As a penalty-saver he was probably second to none. In fact his ability from spot-kicks probably earned him his chance to become an Owl.

Manager Bob Brown attended a trial game during which he pulled off a superb dead-ball save. Other credentials were evident from his debut when he kept a clean sheet against Bristol City. A true gentleman, he managed to temper his competitive element well and only ever showed a sign of annoyance once. Incandescent with rage he chased a referee complaining that Sheffield United's Joe Kitchen had put the ball through goal with his hand during a tense game. Despite Davison's reputation the official remained unmoved though many others were swayed by the sheer sight of this particular keeper in protest. Davison is currently the sixth oldest England debutant. At 34 years and 192 days he was called upon to represent his country against Wales in March 1922.

SMALL CHANGE

Wednesday boss Bob Brown was forced to eat a huge slice of humble pie when his side were on the receiving end of a 5–1 thrashing by Darlington in the spring of 1925. Not too long before this game Brown had dismissed Quakers' winger Mark Hooper due to his lack of height. The player told the Wednesday boss that he hoped to prove him wrong in a match against Sheffield Wednesday and with two goals and a superb all-round performance he certainly did that. Hooper also contributed to Darlington strolling to the Third Division North title. Standing at a mere 5ft 6in he didn't have the usual stature of a professional footballer and certainly not his position (nor indeed that of goalkeeper where he started out as an aspiring junior). While he may have appeared something of a lightweight this was far from the truth. In January 1927 he signed for the Owls in exchange for a sum totalling just under £2,000. There was an element of strategic planning by the Feethams club who were leaking goals as they battled to evade relegation from Division Two. A desire to shore up their defence saw them use Hooper's transfer fee and a little extra to land Jimmy Waugh from Sheffield United.

Proof of Hooper's robust nature comes by his remaining an ever-present over three whole seasons from 1928 to 1931. During this time he worked in tandem with Ellis Rimmer with whom he probably formed the best wing partnership of his generation. To this day Hooper's 189 consecutive league and cup games stand as a club record. This spell included Wednesday's back-to-back championship campaigns during which he contributed a healthy number of goals. Though not a prolific scorer in statistical terms he could boast a return of 136 strikes from 423 games for Wednesday and had a habit of grabbing vital strikes including a hat-trick against Tottenham during the great escape mounted against relegation to the Second Division towards the end of the 1927/28 campaign.

ALL ABOARD THE SHOWBOAT

Franck Songo'o made an impact late in his debut on loan from Portsmouth during the spring of 2008. With the Owls leading Queens Park Rangers 2–1, and the game just seconds away from ending, he tried the 'rainbow kick' – more classically known as the Lambretta. This involved stepping over the ball he was in possession of, then clipping it over his head (in the trajectory of a rainbow shape) with a flick from the trailing leg. Players from the London club surrounded the Cameroonian forcibly suggesting that he had shown a lack of professional respect. QPR's Hogan Ephraim was dismissed during the ensuing melee for suggested use of an elbow.

DREAM DEBUTS

In terms of impact on debut it would be hard to top the feat of Lloyd Owusu who netted within a minute of his introduction to the Sheffield derby during September 2002. Owusu's first touch of the game and his Wednesday career was a header which opened the scoring 17 minutes from time and paved the way to a 2–0 home win.

SEEING RED

John McIntyre was transformed from hero to villain in the space of a minute when, against Birmingham in 1921, he was sent off moments after converting a penalty. His crime was retaliation to the incident which led to the spot-kick.

Tom Cawley was embroiled in a strange sending-off. The epitome of a gentleman player, he was stunned at being asked to leave the field against Lincoln in 1888. His disciplinary record had been untarnished until that time and such a reaction seemed to stun the referee who decided to retract his decision after realising an error had been made. However, despite invitations to rejoin the game Cawley steadfastly refused on a matter of principle.

One of the most notorious sendings-off during recent years is that of Paulo Di Canio who, after a fracas with Arsenal's Martin Keown, was dismissed in a league game and pushed referee Paul Alcock. The official was sent reeling and eventually sank to the ground in a pronounced, overly dramatic fashion. The Italian, hit by a massive 11-game ban and fined, never appeared for the club again, transferring to West Ham United in a cut-price deal after refusing to attend training once the sanction ended. Di Canio, who not only clashed with Keown but had a lesser altercation with Nigel Winterburn as he left the field, was no stranger to opprobrium and received a £1,000 for 'mooning' after scoring against Wimbledon not long after his arrival at Hillsborough. However, just over two years later an act of sportsmanship won a FIFA Fair Play Award. The Italian opted to catch a cross rather than execute the simple task of knocking the ball in with the keeper lying prone and in need of attention inside the area.

KNIVES OFTEN OUT IN THE STEEL CITY

Rivalry between the Sheffield clubs has been intensified by a number of high-profile games and the fact that on many occasions both have been chasing the same prize. At the end of the 1938/39 season the Owls and Blades vied for Division Two's final promotion place. United lay one point behind Wednesday but needed a win over Spurs to pip their neighbours on the line. A draw would not be enough as Wednesday had the superior goal average. The Owls had completed their programme a week earlier beating Spurs who were powerless to resist the Blades and received a 6–1 hammering.

To level matters, United missed out by just 0.008 of a goal when Tottenham, runaway champions of the second tier, earned a 0–0 draw with Wednesday on the final day of the 1949/50 season. That result saw the Blades leapfrogged. A 1–1 draw would have put the Sheffield clubs level on not just points but goal average. Under competition rules a one-off match would have decided the runners-up spot.

BATTLE OF BRAMALL LANE

Some bad blood during the early years of Wednesday v United contests could be put down to the defection of players when the Blades were formed, but antipathy was never more evident than in an FA Cup second round game in February 1900 and the 'Battle of Bramall Lane'. The match had been eagerly anticipated and that sense was heightened when the first scheduled game was abandoned after 50 minutes owing to a snowstorm. The rescheduled encounter was also postponed in blizzard-like conditions. Bramall Lane finally got through the 90 minutes at the third time of asking with the teams drawing 1–1. This was a bad-tempered affair. Most players who made it through the entire game limped from the field and some were unavailable for the rematch due to injury, although Wednesday's George Lee fell victim to the elements rather than a bad challenge having to be carried off with a broken leg suffered after a hefty fall.

Moods had not calmed during the intervening week and through a combination of injury and sendings off United finished with nine men and Wednesday eight. John Pryce and Ambrose Langley were given their marching orders for putting George Hedley and Walter Bennett out of the game as the sides waged war. United won 2–0 but as cup holders and leaders of the First Division were clear favourites to go through, despite the Owls being in similar form and topping Division Two. Their numerical advantage also told. A challenge by Langley on Bennett before his dismissal actually set United on their way as it allowed Ernest Needham to successfully convert a penalty.

CUTTING YOUR LOSSES

Paolo Di Canio's sale to West Ham United less than 18 months after arriving at Hillsborough was for a fee £2.5 million less than the record price Wednesday acquired the Italian for. Andy Booth joined for £2.7 million in 1996. Five years later, after some injuries derailed his promising early form, he returned to Huddersfield Town with just £200,000 changing hands.

SUMMER OF THE LONG KNIVES

Wednesday's disappointing 2002/03 relegation season was greeted by a mass clear-out as manager Chris Turner told thirteen players they no longer had a future at the club and were free to go. The departing bunch included some who were out of contract but also established names such as Ashley Westwood, Tony Crane, captain Trond-Egil Soltvedt and Steve Haslam who Turner later resigned at Hartlepool United.

GONE IN 13 SECONDS

Wednesday's keepers had a distinguished disciplinary record until the beginning of the 2000/01 campaign when Kevin Pressman wrote himself into history with the then quickest dismissal from the start of a game in league history. During the season's opening fixture with Wolves he was sent off for handling outside his area just 13 seconds into the game. A further five Owls players received yellow cards before the afternoon was out – primarily due to that controversial decision. The keeper maintained his innocence insisting he chested rather than handled the ball. However, the Football League ruled that no appeal was possible unless referee Mark Halsey mistook his identity – which was out of the question – or there were cases of violent conduct and serious foul play.

KICKING-OFF

On making his exit as a substitute from the Sheffield derby in October 2008, Jermaine Johnson became one of few players to be sent off while not on the field of play. Reacting with what may be termed as extreme disappointment to his replacement 22 minutes from time by Akpo Sodje, he collected a second yellow card, then the subsequent red, for kicking a water bottle into the crowd.

BEATEN BY THE WHISTLEBLOWER

A goal scored by Jack Allen in the semi-final of the 1929/30 FA Cup was ruled out as the ball crossed the line after the referee had blown for time. Huddersfield Town led 2–1 at that point so progressed to the final despite their late scare.

IN THE FAMILY WAY

Playing for Wednesday has been something of a family affair virtually since the club was founded. Tom Brandon was the cousin of Harry Brandon and saw his brothers Jim and Bob play for Wednesday. Jim McCalliog's brother Fred (who moved from London with other family members when his sibling joined the Owls), was with the club for a short time but never made the first team. Jim McAnearney was another outshone by his brother Tom who played almost 400 games for the club. Like his brother, Tom made his debut against Liverpool but that is where the similarity in their Wednesday careers ends. Jim managed just a tenth of that total but was able to line-up with his sibling 26 times. Peter Shirtliff was another to make far more appearances than his brother Paul who only spent a few years at Hillsborough compared to his older sibling's decade as a Wednesday player when his two spells with the club are combined.

Added to the ranks of brothers with lopsided Owls careers are Tom and Percy Crawshaw. The former is one of the club's leading appearance makers while Percy gained just 9 senior chances. Alan and Brian Finney enjoy similar status although the former didn't make the first XI – nor did David Mobley while his brother Vic made more than 200 appearances. Chris Hooper could not attain the same standards his brother Mark set while Tom Brelsford made over 100 senior outings contrasted to Ben and Charles, both left-backs who found Jim Blair impossible to dislodge. Albert Quixall was at one stage the costliest footballer in Britain while George only had a brief stint as a professional and a briefer stay at Hillsborough. Richard Wood's brother Nick was another unable to follow a lead and both left the club during 2010. Richard went to Coventry City after almost 200 Wednesday outings while his younger brother sought academy terms elsewhere.

Ron Springett saw his sibling Peter play for the club but in a unique situation. Both started their careers at Queens Park Rangers but in May 1967, after a decade at Hillsborough, the former returned to Loftus Road in a deal which brought his brother travelling in the other direction. Peter was valued at £40,000 while Ron offset that by £16,000. The two may never have turned out for the same team but did oppose each other twice while at Hillsborough and Loftus Road respectively. Wednesday won both matches.

There are two other distinctive events; twins turned out for the same Wednesday team when Derek and Eric Wilkinson were selected together for the first and only time in September 1958 for a game against Sunderland. This outing was Eric's sole appearance for the club. Jack and Laurie Burkinshaw are the only brothers to score in the same game for the Owls. They achieved this in a 3–0 home defeat of Chelsea on Boxing Day 1913.

Both Charles and William Clegg played for Wednesday following the club's formation. While Charles went on to become a referee upon retiring, William stayed connected by joining the club's board. He served as chairman then President and took similar roles within the Football Association. Other brothers who have been on Wednesday's books are Tom and Len Armitage, Arnold and Wally Birch, Carl and Darren Bradshaw, Ted and Tom Buttery, Carl and Walpole Hiller, Leon and Rocky Lekaj, Brian and John Linighan, Bezek, Kazimirez and Stanislaw Nowakowski plus Jamie and Michael Simpkins. The tally of siblings would have been added to if Brian Laws had been successful in gaining the signature of Sam Sodje alongside his brother Akpo in August 2007. While the latter was quickly snaffled from Port Vale after an excellent performance against the Owls in pre-season, negotiations to land Sam from Reading proved lengthy. A host of problems failed to be ironed out prior to the transfer window closing.

LIKE FATHER, LIKE SON

Just a handful of fathers and sons have been with Wednesday. Don Megson proved to be a stalwart member of the first team line-up between 1959 and 1970. His son Gary spent eight years at Hillsborough when his two stints are added together. He is currently adding to that tally as first-team manager. One of Megson's predecessors in the hotseat, Danny Wilson, also spent time at Hillsborough during his playing career. His son Laurie had a limited run in the first team before drifting down the league pyramid into Conference football. George Nevin spent time at Wednesday prior to the Second World War. His father Ralph also watched another son David become a professional though his contribution to first-team matters was participation in a County Cup tie with Doncaster Rovers.

More recently, when Neil Mellor signed on a season's loan from Preston North End in 2010 he followed his father Ian, who had three terms at Hillsborough in the late 1970s and early 1980s. A little further back in history, Frank Froggatt and his son Redfern also enjoyed long stints with the Owls between 1921–7 and 1946–60 respectively. Both players captained the club. Though Red's son Paul only made it as far as the youth ranks, he became the third generation of Froggatts to represent Wednesday. A little further along the generation gap Denis Woodhead followed in his grandfather's footsteps when he turned out for Wednesday in 1947. That grandparent was Billy Betts who played for the club in its pre-Football League days.

Trevor Matthewson gained only a few first-team games during the early 1980s. A Sheffield boy, his grandfather Tommy failed to make a senior outing for Wednesday but was part of the South Shields side which caused a huge upset by knocking the Owls out of the FA Cup in February 1927. Trevor's uncle Reg Matthewson spent a decade at Bramall Lane.

Many other players have had members of their family play professional football even if not for Wednesday. John Fantham's dad, Jack, played with Stockport County before the war and Don Gibson was Sir Matt Busby's son-in-law. That relationship became particularly poignant after the Munich Air Disaster as Wednesday – with Gibson in the line-up – were the first team to meet Manchester United when the club returned to playing.

BLUE & WHITE WEDDING

A further Wednesday man with a Manchester United connection, Neil Dewar, left Old Trafford for Hillsborough in 1933 when exchanged for George Nevin and Jack Ball. The 25-year-old had been secretly courting Betty Thomson, daughter of Red Devils board member Mr A.E. Thomson, prior to the transfer. A desire to continue their relationship after he crossed the Pennines led Dewar to propose. Betty accepted and the pair kept their nuptials secret until just after they married on 30 December 1933 – the morning of a Wednesday home game with Manchester City.

The event came a day after the deal was brokered which saw him leave Manchester and his digs close to the Thomson's family home. The pair spent a short honeymoon in London before Dewar rejoined the Owls squad and scored in a 1–1 draw at Highbury. Mr and Mrs Thomson only learned of the relationship, let alone their marriage, after the weekend. Their son, also called Neil, played for Scotland's youth team then Queen's Park and would have gained amateur honours if his Sheffield birthplace had not been enquired into. His father's Lochgilphead upbringing and return to Third Lanark before Dewar junior started school counted for nothing.

ON THE RIGHT TRACK

Stories of deals for players being struck at motorway service stations became commonplace during the 1990s but Wednesday's agreement to buy Billy Felton was essentially made on a train. On 1 January 1923 the defender travelled north with his Grimsby Town team-mates expecting to play in a Third Division North tie with Accrington Stanley. As the train ground to a halt at Sheffield he was asked to disembark and report to Hillsborough so he could sign for the Owls. He made one of the quickest debuts in history playing against Southampton that same afternoon. The game finished 0–0 but his new club benefitted from the partnership Felton would form with Ernest Blenkinsop which blossomed and earned each international honours along with plaudits from their peers. The arrival of Tommy Walker hastened his departure with run-outs limited to the odd stint when one or the other first-choice full-back was injured. He left Hillsborough to join Manchester City in 1929.

Fred Spiksley was another to find rail transport to Accrington crucial in a signing. His train journey from Gainsborough was unexpectedly delayed at Sheffield where he met Wednesday directors John Holmes and Fred Thompson. Spiksley had asked for time to consider a switch to Accrington FC but the Wednesday pair persuaded him to call off the transfer he was now due to complete at the other end and come to the Olive Grove instead. It was a good piece of business as the striker was top scorer in each of his first couple of seasons. Two years after his arrival in January 1891 the striker hit his first hat-trick for the club in an FA Cup win over Derby County. This was also the first scored by any Wednesday player at Owlerton.

LET THERE BE LIGHT

Like most clubs, Wednesday set about installing floodlights during the 1950s. They were officially unveiled in March 1955 and first used for Derek Dooley's benefit match against an International XI. 55,000 spectators turned out to pay not only money but respect to a man who had all his dreams snatched from him as a result of that fateful challenge two years earlier. £7,500 was raised and that attendance actually surpassed the number who were present to see the illuminations first used in a league game on 21 March 1956 when Barnsley were the visitors. 31,577 attended to see Wednesday pull off a 3–0 win.

CUSHIONS & THROWS

In order to add a little comfort for denizens of the North Stand, cushions were on offer for a small fee courtesy of the supporters' club. However, this gesture caused Wednesday to receive a £100 fine when many of the padded items were thrown on to the field after David Layne was dismissed during a goalless draw with Aston Villa – the match was one Wednesday were disappointed not to have wrapped up before their striker was red-carded. There was a lesser incident 17 years later after which the opportunity for fans to cushion their bottoms against the seats was withdrawn.

A LONG, LONG SEASON

Four replays against eventual winners Arsenal in the 1978/79 FA Cup went some way to establishing a club record for the highest number of games within a single season. Wednesday played 59 first-team matches; 46 as part of their Third Division campaign, 9 in the FA Cup (each game in the three rounds contested went to at least one replay) and 4 in the League Cup. In the latter competition an extra match was needed against Doncaster Rovers as two legs could not produce a winner. That brought the overall minutes played to a massive 5,400.

WADDLE PROVES WRITE ON

Chris Waddle became to the first and so far only Wednesday player to claim the accolade of Football Writers' Association Player of the Year Award in recognition of his form during the 1992/93 campaign.

FROM THE BENCH

Rules allowing the replacement of injured players or tactical changes during a game are a relatively modern innovations. Substitutes were allowed to sit on the bench from 21 August 1965. Wednesday first used the new legislation by introducing David Ford for Don Megson on 23 October. Jack Whitham became the first number 12 to score after coming on the field in a 7–0 home win over Burnley on 6 May 1967.

KEEPERS OF THE FAITH

The highly specialised position of goalkeeper is one which enjoys a special place within the club's rich history and usually in the hearts of fans. Jack Brown has made the most appearances for Wednesday between the sticks with 507 outings. Bob Bolder has the best games to goals conceded average – 243 strikes made their way past him over the 224 games he played which works out to a meagre 1.08 goals per game. Three players hold the record for the most clean sheets over a league campaign with 16 shut-outs. They are Jack Lyall in 1903/04, Jack Brown during the 1925/26 campaign and Martin Hodge in 1983/84.

Away from the aggrandisement of Wednesday's great custodians, Hodge has a unique and unfortunate distinction which separates him from all his peers – conceding to his opposite number. In October 1986 Coventry City's Steve Ogrizovic lofted a goal-kick which found Hodge too far off his line. Despite a desperate scramble to make up ground, the ball lobbed over the stricken number one before bouncing over the line and securing a 2–2 draw.

No Wednesday keeper had scored until 23 December 2006 when Mark Crossley netted an equaliser against Southampton after coming up for a last-gasp corner at Hillsborough.

Had it not been for the form of Teddy Davison, his understudy, Arnold Birch, could well have became the first to keeper to net. Birch scored a number of goals at the various clubs he served from the penalty spot. After leaving Wednesday he scored 5 for Chesterfield over the 1923/24 season.

IN WHERE IT HURTS

A keeper to face adversity in the Wednesday goal is Frank Stubbs. He spent just under two seasons with the club but lost his place after being kicked in the head during a game against Notts County in September 1901. Played well before the days of substitutes, the hapless custodian was forced to continue but rather than stick him out on the wing as teams normally did with keepers, Stubbs was left to guard the net. Clearly dazed he let in 6 goals, a few of which his counterparts would have easily stopped.

MR VERSATILITY

Players are often described as utility men, some even earn the accolade Mr Versatility. If any Wednesday man deserves that tag it is Lee Bullen. After converting himself from a striker to a central defender midway through an itinerant career which had postings in his native Scotland, Australia, Greece plus the upper and lower echelons of Hong Kong football, he turned up at Hillsborough after helping Dunfermline Athletic reach the 2004 Scottish Cup final. Along with the captain's armband during that first season there were a number of briefs. In the next term he achieved the feat of representing the Owls in eleven different positions within a single campaign. Prior to a match with Millwall during early February 2006 he had been asked to play in all outfield roles, then an injury forced keeper David Lucas off just before half time. Wednesday didn't have a deputy on the bench and Bullen was thrown the gloves. The Londoners thought they had beaten the stand-in direct from a corner early in the second period only to see their goal disallowed. The Owls took their free-kick quickly and poured upfield while some Lions' players were still celebrating. American Frank Simek slammed the ball in after a scramble close to the line. Bullen who looked accomplished in the simple tasks tipped a David Livermore effort onto the bar, then over. His performance ensured Wednesday took the maximum advantage from the proverbial relegation six-pointer. At the end of season PFA Awards, the Scot carried home the Good Sport accolade.

PLAYING UNDER A PSEUDONYM

An interesting footnote to the career of Jim Smith, a keeper with Wednesday between 1884 and 1893, is that he preferred to play under this name than his real moniker Jim Clarke. Some other Owls players have changed their names. Neumünster-born Wilf Smith was only so called as his family chose to anglicise their Schmidt surname when moving from Germany. The Second World War was not long over and his parents were keen to fit in. Wilf skippered Sheffield Boys and England at youth level.

David Cusack was born Rodrigo Jair David Cusack-Menezes. There was a large influence from his Brazilian dad and Jair was bestowed as a middle name due this heritage plus in tribute to Jairzinho, a 1970 World Cup-winner. A grandfather on his maternal side of the family was named David. This and his Mother's maiden name, Cusack, made sure he didn't stand out too much as a lad in Rotherham.

BRING YOUR OWN GOALPOSTS

Huddersfield RLFC's Fartown Ground was selected as the neutral venue at which Wednesday would take on Blackburn Rovers in the 1882 FA Cup semi-final. The area had little if any footballing pedigree and Huddersfield Town would not be formed until 1908. Rugby League was the sport of choice as demonstrated by the fact that Wednesday supplied the goalposts. Not that they were needed in the end as the match finished scoreless. The replay at Fallowfield, Manchester, – to which neither side had to contribute any fixtures or fittings – saw Blackburn triumph 5–1.

GOALS, GOALS, GOALS

Douglas Hunt holds the record for scoring the most goals in a single game with 6 in a Second Division meeting with Norwich City on 19 November 1938. The striker had managed 4 against Rotherham United in a County Cup game – a competition all senior sides took seriously at the time – and netted in a 5–1 defeat at West Bromwich Albion seven days earlier. Jackie Robinson laid on 5 of Hunt's goals against Norwich. Bill Fallon provided the other for the day's hero and took a further slice of the plaudits by notching himself in the 7–0 win. A week on and the forward struck what was essentially his third hat-trick in a week by hitting a treble at Luton Town.

Five players have scored 5 in a game but only Jimmy Trotter has managed the feat twice.

Derek Dooley	3/11/1951	v Notts County	Div 2
Jimmy Dailey	6/9/1947	v Barnsley	Div 2
Jimmy Trotter	21/9/1925	v Stockport C	Div 2
Jimmy Trotter	13/12/1924	v Portsmouth	Div 2
Toddles Woolhouse	17/1/1891	v Halliwell	FA Cup
Bob Gregory	4/11/1882	v Spilsby	FA Cup

Jack Allen once struck 7 for the reserves though heavy scoring for the second string does not constitute an official record.

Over the course of an entire season Derek Dooley bagged 47 from just 30 games during 1951/52 which helped the club run away with the Second Division championship. This mark created a divisional record which stands to this day – 50 years later he was presented with a golden boot to mark the achievement.

FORTRESS HILLSBOROUGH

Wednesday are one of just nine clubs to go through an entire league campaign not only unbeaten at home but having claimed a 100 per cent record. The 17 matches won during the 1899/1900 season helped the Owls climb out of the Second Division. Prior to the Premier League era this had been achieved just six times in 104 years and on all but one occasion from a shorter campaign than that historic first season at Hillsborough. Having been defeated in the final game at the Olive Grove by Newcastle United, the record of continuous victories is stretched to 19 games when wins over Bolton Wanderers and Notts County at the beginning of the next season are counted. Preston North End were the first team to return from S6 without a defeat courtesy of their 1–0 victory. Wednesday have remained unbeaten at home during three other league campaigns: in 1903/04, 1928/29 and 1934/35.

Between 27 December 1902, when the Owls beat Notts County, and a 3–0 win over Stoke on 15 October 1904, an unbeaten sequence of 31 home games without defeat had been strung together. Arsenal ended that streak in some style sweeping Wednesday aside 3–0.

Although the Owls lost points and matches at home over 74 games between 21 September 1929 and 2 January 1933, they were able to register at least a goal per game. A scoreless draw with Derby County ended that impressive sequence.

UNBEATABLE

Wednesday's best run of consecutive league victories are the 9 games from 23 April to 15 October 1904, during which time 26 goals were scored and just 6 conceded. The early 1960s saw the club establish a record for a string of games without defeat. From 10 December 1960 to 8 April 1961 Wednesday went 19 games without losing. Away from home a string of 6 straight wins from 28 April to 6 October 1990 constitute the club's best run. The unbeaten record for games not at Hillsborough stands at 11 matches played from 10 November 1979 to 5 April 1980.

A run of 7 draws between 15 March and 14 April 2008, 4 of which came at Hillsborough, provided vital points in a bid to break free of relegation trouble and retain Championship status. However, with the Owls in 22nd place – the second tier's third space in the drop zone – progress to safety was agonisingly slow. The sequence began at Coventry City and 4 games in, a rearranged match against the same opposition at Hillsborough saw that share of the spoils allow a limp forward by two spots. Defeat at Blackpool ended the run of tied matches and saw Wednesday drop back right where they started. Fortunately a couple of wins in the season's last 2 games banished any spectre of demotion.

STARS IN STRIPES

The most successful early US soccer import to hit these shores, John Harkes, cost just £70,000 from American Soccer League outfit Albany Capitals. Despite a preference for midfield roles he initially played at right-back but eventually found himself flitting around the pitch giving great value in any department required. In his first term he helped the club achieve both League Cup success and win promotion to Division One. Two seasons later he returned to Wembley as Wednesday vied to claim the League Cup for the second time in three years, Harkes netting after 9 minutes. Many believed the man from a part of New Jersey colloquially known as Soccer Town to be the first American to play and score at Wembley. However, that distinction belongs to Bill Regan who represented Romford in the 1949 FA Amateur Cup final and, professionally, Mike Masters who netted for Colchester United in the 1992 FA Trophy final. In the summer of 1993 Derby County offered £500,000 for the services of Harkes, who was held as a hero across the Atlantic. To date, the only other American national to pull on a blue and white striped shirt is Frank Simek.

A WELL-TRAVELLED AMATEUR

Mike Pinner was a part-time footballer who usually earned his living as a solicitor. At weekends he played in local leagues near his Lincolnshire birthplace. However, his talents did not go unnoticed by professional clubs. Notts County were the first to offer a chance after seeing him turn out for youth side Wyberton. Pinner never made it past the reserves at Meadow Lane due to his studies and the advent of the Second World War, although he represented the RAF and won a 'blue' at Cambridge University, playing in 4 Varsity games held at Wembley. Aston Villa lured him from the highly regarded Pegasus amateur side and provided a first taste of league football. Sheffield Wednesday followed after a brief spell with Corinthian Casuals and then came Queens Park Rangers, Manchester United, Chelsea, Swansea Town and Leyton Orient, with whom he turned professional at the age of 28. A season with Lisburn Distillery saw him hang up those well-travelled gloves in 1966. Pinner also represented Great Britain in successive Olympics – the 1956 tournament in Melbourne and four years later in Rome.

TREBLE CHANCE

Jimmy Trotter has struck the most hat-tricks in Wednesday's history and his seven Football League trebles were scored over three seasons. David McLean weighs in with six hat-tricks. Jack Allen, Derek Dooley and Mark Hooper have all notched five. Dooley's record is particularly remarkable given that they were hit in the space of just over a year.

Bob Gregory struck Wednesday's first hat-trick in top-grade football against Blackburn Rovers on 18 December 1880 in the FA Cup. Alec Brady claimed the club's first treble in the Football League on 14 October 1893 during a Division One game with Derby County. In other competitions, the honour of grabbing the Owls' first League Cup hat-trick goes to Roger Wylde who scored 3 against Doncaster Rovers in the League Cup on 13 August 1977. In Europe Gerry Young hit 3 against no less a team than Roma at Hillsborough on 29 November 1961 during the club's first foray into the Fairs Cup. Only one other player has notched a European hat-trick – David Layne in a 4–1 home win over DOS Utrecht.

Ted Harper is the sole man to claim a treble on debut. That came in a 6–4 win over Derby County on 18 February 1927. Andy Blair became the first and so far only player in Wednesday's history to score a hat-trick of penalties during a 4–2 League Cup win over Luton Town in November 1984.

THREE & OUT

Frank Bradshaw's impressive goalscoring form earned a call-up for England in June 1908. The striker netted a hat-trick in an 11–1 win against Austria – a feat made all the more impressive by the beaten team being hosts. The following spring Bradshaw was selected to face Ireland but withdrew as a result of injury. Never invited to represent his country again, he is one of just five England players to grab a treble on what turned out to be both his debut and last international appearance.

INJURED AT WORK

Though a short-lived career by definition, the physical nature of professional football means playing days can be shortened even further by the human body's limitations. Billy Marsden had his career wrecked by injury though not while on duty for Wednesday. An accidental clash with team-mate Roy Goodall in May 1930 when England took on Germany in Berlin injured the left-half's spine. Recovery was always likely to be an uphill struggle and the evidence of a few reserve games bore this out.

Similarly there is no knowing exactly what Hugh Swift could have achieved but for the Second World War and a double fracture to his jaw suffered in February 1950. Despite beginning his time at Hillsborough in a forward role he was switched to defence in 1943 and rewarded with a professional contract once the war was ended. 132 consecutive appearances had been racked up by the time he received the injury. A return was attempted the following season but medical advice forced him to finish not long after.

Eddie Kilshaw was a young player who saw his dreams come to nothing just 19 games into his Wednesday career when sustaining a dislocated knee in April 1949. The world seemed at his feet just months earlier when he attracted a record £20,000 fee for a winger.

SEVEN DAYS LATER

A 'flu epidemic led Wednesday to start the 1957/58 term a week later than their rivals. Whether the bug lingered on is a moot point – the Owls were relegated after finishing bottom of the First Division.

AND LATER STILL

Wednesday completed their 1946/47 season on 7 June. It was the first proper league campaign staged after the Second World War and originally had a scheduled completion date of 26 April. This had to be scrapped when Government regulations banned previously postponed matches being arranged during midweek. A game at Chesterfield's Saltergate stadium rounded off a fairly disappointing campaign in which Wednesday narrowly missed dropping down to Division Three.

LEAGUE CUP

Although the League Cup came into being in 1960, Wednesday didn't deem it worthy of participation until the 1966/67 season. Many clubs passed up on the opportunity to enter over its early years with the competition only really catching on when teams realised that it could be an early-season moneyspinner. A place in Europe for the winners coming on offer around that time also helped. Wednesday entertained Rotherham United in their first ever tie. The Second Division side were beaten finalists in the first League Cup final and maintained their impressive record by scoring the only goal of the game. At one stage Wednesday's record in the competition was far from ideal. Fifth round berths (equivalent to the quarter-final stage) over three successive seasons from 1982 to 1985 were as good as it got. Despite this, Wednesday had one of the best records in the competition over the 1990s reaching two finals and a couple of semi-finals. Only one player, Nigel Pearson in 1991, has won the Man of the Match award – the Alan Hardaker Trophy.

WAR OF THE MONSTER TRUCKS

The club's debut League Cup final in 1991 was the first time the cup had been contested under sponsorship by electrical retailers Rumbelows whose Employee of the Year, Tracy Bateman, was given the honour of handing over the silverware. Despite impressive progress being made to Wembley, Division Two Wednesday were second favourites to Manchester United – well established in the top flight and also FA Cup holders. However, John Sheridan's goal sealed a deserved victory. Although broadcast live on national television, those Wednesday fans unable to get a ticket were denied the chance to see Nigel Pearson receive and then lift the trophy as Yorkshire TV quickly switched away from the action other ITV regions stayed with, choosing to show *War of the Monster Trucks*.

Two years later Wednesday were back to face Arsenal. Again the trophy bore new sponsors – Coca Cola. Unfortunately Wednesday's fizz deserted them as the Gunners edged to a 2–1 victory and since that last appearance at Wembley in 1993, Wednesday have struggled to make an impact although they did reach the last four during the 2001/02 campaign. The Football League's only representatives fancied their chances against Blackburn Rovers who were struggling to keep Premier League status but lost to the eventual winners over two legs.

TV HIGHLIGHTS

Recorded highlights of games played over a weekend became a popular feature during the 1960s. *Match of the Day* cameras captured Wednesday for the first time in FA Cup action – a third round clash with Everton on 9 January 1965. John Fantham and John Quinn hogged the limelight at Goodison Park with the match something of a classic which finished 2–2.

WEDNESDAY EVERY DAY OF THE WEEK

Broadcast rights are not the only influence on football being played each day of the week. Scheduled midweek games and public holidays meant matches have fallen on various days. However, the Sabbath was sacrosanct until restrictions on the use of power and a three-day week introduced during the 1974 miners' strike led the football authorities to introduce Sunday kick-offs. These limited the effects industrial action had on the smooth running of fixture lists. Wednesday played their first ever Sunday match on 10 February 1974 when Bristol City were defeated 3–1. A healthy crowd – well up on recent home attendances – made the experiment a financial success.

A SPOT OF TROUBLE

Over the course of the 1977/78 campaign ten Wednesday players missed penalties and a horrendous seven spot-kicks were spurned in succession. During the 1983/84 season Wednesday were having a similarly horrendous time until Mel Sterland broke the run against Barnsley on 5 November. Little more than a decade earlier no Wednesday man had a chance to so much as miss a penalty. A run of 81 games from Boxing Day 1964, when Colin Dobson fired in an early spot-kick, passed until a referee next pointed to the spot in the Owls' favour on 1 October 1966. Just two minutes remained when Peter Eustace gave a hammering at Southampton a little respectability and made it 4–2.

In a youth tournament during 1996 the Owls' junior side lost a penalty shoot-out to their counterparts from St Etienne 1–0. It's a rare event for a shoot-out to be so tight. Even less regularly does this happen after the first five attempts each side had before sudden death were spurned.

While those who miss spot-kicks are often considered zeroes, the goalkeeper becomes a hero when a penalty taker is foiled. Although Wednesday have boasted some of the best men between their posts for these particular battles of wit, Peter Grummitt deserves an honourable mention for saving a twice-taken penalty against Oxford United early in the 1970/71 campaign. He stooped low to deny Brian Thompson midway through the second half only for the officials to decide they had seen movement before the ball was struck.

Although he would have beaten many stoppers with the kick, Thompson decided he should not have responsibility for the retake. That passed to Colin Clarke who struck the ball equally as well as his team-mate but Grummitt once more flung himself towards its course and pulled off another miraculous stop. The Owls led 1–0 at the time and though those efforts seemed set to win both points, it actually only saved the one as Oxford grabbed a late equaliser.

NO SIGN OF NERVES

Colin Gregson got precious little chance at Hillsborough. Signed just ahead of the manager who drafted him being asked to leave, he was a decent performer in the reserves but that failed to cut much ice. As a youngster in the North-East he showed little nerve from the penalty spot or fear of occasion. Before ITV cameras at St James' Park the then 14-year-old successfully converted 6 of 10 penalty kicks in a competition which was not only televised but pitted him against Newcastle United's first choice keeper Ian McFaul – an experienced professional not to mention an international.

NEVER GO BACK

Marlon Beresford joined Wednesday as a youngster but failed to make a first-team appearance before joining Burnley. Almost 10 years after his departure, the keeper was loaned to the Owls as cover and finally made a long-awaited debut – unfortunately in a 2–0 defeat by Blackburn Rovers. Middlesbrough were his parent club at that time. The phrase never go back has been largely ignored by the stopper who has had three stints at Turf Moor plus a couple at Northampton Town (both temporary transfers during his Sheffield days) and Luton Town.

SHOOT-OUT

The first tie involving Wednesday to be decided on penalties was in the opening round of the 1975/76 League Cup. Darlington lay a division lower than the Owls but managed to hold out for a draw. A penalty shoot-out followed which the North-East side won with ease.

New rules introduced in 1994 limited FA Cup games to a single replay. Should the scores remain level after a subsequent 30 minutes extra time, a tie would be decided by spot-kicks. The Owls lost their first such showdown in February 1995 to Wolves 4–2 despite leading by three clear penalties. Mark Bright, Guy Whittingham and Kevin Pressman were the men who had seemingly secured passage to the fifth round only for Andy Pearce and Chris Bart-Williams to miss their efforts while the Old Gold's fortunes picked up. In sudden death Chris Waddle, who had a penalty saved in England's 1990 World Cup semi-final defeat with West Germany, saw his jinx continue when Mike Stowell saved a nervous effort. Don Goodman put Wolves through. In that shoot-out Pressman cracked home one of the sweetest penalties any player had dispatched all season. Wednesday were having something of a nightmare run when it came to spot-kicks and fuelled by that cool dispatch into the top right-hand corner plus the self-confidence which hallmarks most keepers, Kevin promptly volunteered to take all the penalties Wednesday may be awarded for the rest of the season. There is no evidence to substantiate claims to this being a factor in him being dropped in favour of Chris Woods for a spell soon after that offer.

Three years on against Watford in an FA Cup third round replay Pressman repeated the trick of saving and scoring penalties in a shoot-out. This time he claimed the winner after denying Micah Hyde to make the score 4–3 ahead of the last round of kicks. Pressman stepped forward smashing the ball high past Alec Chamberlain. A trio of saves saw Wednesday beat Crystal Palace in the shoot-out to decide progress to meet Aston Villa in the 2001/02 Worthington Cup.

Wednesday have rarely enjoyed luck with spot-kicks in the FA Cup and were forced to pay the price for not converting two penalties awarded in a third round tie with Glossop North End in 1909. The match was staged at Hillsborough so the majority of the crowd were also left to rue those gilt-edged chances and the horror of giving one away which the visitors duly converted to win 1–0.

ON THE BALL

Jack Ball was one of the best penalty takers the Owls have ever had. By the close of the 1931/32 season he had amassed a creditable 23 goals, 11 of which came from the spot. This set a Football League record for the greatest number of penalties successfully converted in a single season which remained unsurpassed for 40 years. Norman Curtis, a full-back by trade, was rather unusual though highly effective from the spot. He would get a colleague to place the ball which he would then begin to charge at from inside his own half. At full pelt he would hammer an effort goalwards. Remarkably he saved two penalties against Preston North End while deputising for Dave McIntosh early in the 1953/54 campaign. With the Lancastrians leading 1–0, McIntosh broke his arm and though he soldiered on for a while, was forced off for treatment. Curtis was thrown the goalie's jersey and saved a first-half penalty from Tom Finney. Although beaten a couple more times he denied Jimmy Baxter from the game's second spot-kick. However, by the whistle Deepdale was celebrating a 6–0 home victory.

UPS …

Wednesday have achieved ten promotions. After losing top-flight status in 1898/99 a leap back was made at the first time of asking. Consistent form for most of a 20-year stay in Division One kept Wednesday away from the trap door but when that run ended the Owls found bouncing back a little trickier. Many teams were fancied to beat Wednesday to promotion at the start of the 1925/26 season. However, despite a sticky patch around Easter the Owls actually managed to secure the Second Division crown by a considerable margin.

In the years just prior to the Second World War Wednesday found the going particularly hard and eventually lost their place among the elite in 1937. There was to be no return until the battle against Hitler's Germany was won. Promotion was achieved once more at the close of the 1949/50 campaign by one of the smallest goal differences ever recorded – 0.0008 of a goal over Sheffield United. A goalless draw would seal promotion. However, defeat or scoring draw could well see the Blades grab the box seat. As it turned out a 0–0 home draw with Tottenham ended any chance United had. Unfortunately the good times ended as quickly as they began and the following term they were relegated Wednesday were asked to do it all again. Remarkably they obliged, in no small part thanks to the prolific Derek Dooley. This time a three-season stint in the top flight was recorded. Again, when downed, the Owls returned quickly claiming another Second Division title in a free scoring campaign.

Harry Catterick steadied the rocking ship Wednesday had became following those 1950s 'yo-yo years' guiding his side to promotion in 1959 with the highest points tally any Second Division outfit had amassed for 12 years. Catterick was long gone by the time Wednesday achieved their next elevation in 1980, but the fact that it was a narrow escape from the Third Division requiring the right result in the final game is a mark of how far the team had slipped over intervening years. One point to note is that at the turn of the year Wednesday looked unlikely candidates to go up but a string of good results turned the season around.

Four years later Wednesday completed their rehabilitation with a convincing promotion campaign which saw them finish runners-up to Chelsea on goal difference but crucially back in the First Division. There was another drop in 1990 but the Owls came straight back up after a third-place finish.

Just one appearance has been made in the end of season play-offs which now decide a division's last promotion place and it was a winning one, even if a late penalty equaliser and extra time was needed to finally see off 10-man Hartlepool United.

... AND DOWNS

A first drop to the Second Division in 1899 was a bitter pill to swallow but Wednesday's record during that campaign was woeful and included many heavy defeats. Seemingly not able to achieve anything by halves, the Owls finished rock bottom of the table once more when relegated for a second time in 1920. Consistency seemed hard to achieve during another shocking campaign which saw Bob Brown use forty-one players.

With a dozen matches of the 1927/28 season remaining it seemed Wednesday would suffer another humiliating relegation but Brown's side found their form and inspiration just in time to put together an amazing run of results to avoid the drop by achieving a creditable 14th place. Yet the congested nature of the table meant the margin of escape was a mere point. A 1–1 draw at Highbury earned by Jimmy Seed's last-minute strike was pivotal and had seen Wednesday lift just clear of the drop zone for the first time in months. It meant that victory over Aston Villa in the final game of the season would save the Owls and a 2–0 win completed what became known as the 'Great Escape'. Emphasising just how vital that sequence of 8 victories, 3 draws and a single defeat was, Wednesday had been without a win in 5 league games before beating Burnley set up a charge for the line which took in equally impressive victories over Liverpool and 2 wins over Spurs. Perhaps the most remarkable feature of this run was that Wednesday lifted back-to-back league championships over the following two seasons.

While four promotions were achieved in the 1950s, Wednesday were forced to stake claims for a place in the top flight after relegation back to the Second Division in 1950/51,1954/55 and 1957/58.

For the next 11 years there were precious few dalliances with relegation; then in 1970 after the most woeful campaign in the club's history Wednesday were sentenced to another spell in Division Two. There was no quick return this time and the Owls finished no higher than 10th place until the 1974/75 campaign which saw the club win a paltry 5 games and draw 11. Losing 26 matches had an inevitable consequence – a further step down the ladder. Freefall into the Football League's basement division was narrowly avoided after looming large for most of the next term. A single point consigned Aldershot to that fate and Wednesday's escape only came about due to Ken Knighton's vital goal 4 minutes from time in the final league game.

Fortunately Wednesday's fortunes went in the opposite direction. A climb back to the old First Division was made over a decade – only marred by relegation in 1990. After an appalling start the Owls climbed out of trouble but Luton Town's surge during the later part of the season consigned Wednesday to their fate by the narrowest of margins. The season's denouement was a tense affair and at various stages it seemed the Owls were safe. In the penultimate round of fixtures Wednesday won at Charlton and in pre-mobile phone days transistor radios were telling relieved away fans that Luton were scoreless at Crystal Palace. Those without that apex of early 1990s technology relied on The Valley's PA announcer who told those present the Eagles had netted across South London. Celebrations over that last-gasp drama were scotched when the tannoy confirmed a goal had been scored – but by the visitors meaning a tense battle for survival would go to the final day. Anything less than maximum points for Luton would make proceedings at Hillsborough academic but from an early stage, events conspired against Wednesday who fell behind to Nottingham Forest while Luton took a lead at Derby. Brian Clough's men made their gulf in class tell against some tired and dispirited Owls players though when County not only halved their arrears but squared matters, hope returned that Wednesday may just stumble over the line. Luton overcame those setbacks to push ahead once more and though rumours Derby had found another leveller saw relieved Wednesdayites counting their blessings, there had in fact been no addition to the score at the Baseball Ground. A goal difference of 2 sent Wednesday down.

The Owls came straight back up the following season and remained in the top flight until relegation from the Premiership in 2000. Three seasons in the second tier ended with demotion to the third for the first time in more than two decades and just over ten years after finishing third at the highest level – not to mention three appearances in domestic finals over two years. A poor start with 13 defeats from the first half of the campaign and, just as importantly, a mere 2 wins was always likely to prove costly. A strong finish gave only brief hope of a second great escape but with two games left the inevitable happened. Five days later an impressive 7–2 win was recorded at Burnley.

A last demotion came from the Championship in 2010. There was hope until the last day as Crystal Palace, who at one stage stood a chance of a play-off place, had 10 points deducted as a result of entering administration. A last-day meeting at Hillsborough could only end in with a home win if Wednesday were to survive. Palace twice held an advantage and despite Darren Purse scoring 3 minutes from time, the Eagles clung on to secure a 2–2 draw.

MOOR ON SURVIVAL

That narrow escape from entering Division Four in 1976 may also have owed a debt to coach Tommy Toms – a marine commander prior to taking a role in football. In January the players were told they would be taking a walk on Broomhead Moor. During that stroll Toms announced their hike would actually become an overnight stay. Such exercises were common in the military who believe they improved morale, comradeship and offered tangible results in battle. Throwing that into football rather than military perspective, Wednesday had been without a win since Bonfire Night. Winter months on those open plains can be extreme and this was the coldest night of that season so far. Basic provisions, rations and some additional clothing – including ladies' tights – were handed to the players who stuck out the conditions and laughed off suggestions that they lost an impromptu kick-about with the resident sheep. Dave Cusack insisted that game had been won after extra time. The match just after that excursion against Chester City was convincingly decided in the Owls' favour.

GOING DOWN, GOING DOWN, GOING DOWN!

A familiar refrain supporters of teams in trouble hear, just a few seasons ago it was virtually a weekly occurrence for former Sheffield Wednesday forward Lloyd Owusu. The striker began the 2008/09 season with Yeovil Town but with less than a month of the campaign gone, joined Cheltenham on a free. That move to the spa town went well on the pitch. However, the Robins were forced to cut costs and allowed Owusu out on loan to Brighton and Hove Albion. At one stage all three teams could have been relegated from League One. Many a player had represented a couple of teams forced through the trap door when a season ended but turning out for three teams demoted from the same division in one season would have created a exclusive place in the history books. However, the temporary signing, who won the divisional Player of the Month award for April, hit a goal every other game helping the Seagulls survive on the last day after beating Stockport County at the Withdean Stadium. Yeovil also got themselves clear of danger, although with a bit more room to spare. Cheltenham were not so lucky.

One player has been a part of three relegated squads in the same season. Junior Agogo started the 1999/2000 term at Hillsborough but with just a few substitute appearances over the previous couple of seasons, was struggling to make an impact. Plenty of non-Premiership clubs were keen to sample what he had to offer and loan spells at Oldham Athletic, Chester City, Chesterfield and Lincoln City were arranged. The Ghanaian international had mixed fortunes in those postings but was a huge success at Chester and deemed to have scored one of the best ever goals at the Deva Stadium. Unfortunately his efforts over two months were not enough to save the Cesterians dropping out of the Football League – although that occurred well after his departure. Chesterfield exited Division Two – the then third tier – after finishing rock-bottom and of course Wednesday bid a sad farewell to the Premiership that season.

THAT SINKING FEELING

Carlton Palmer rose to become a top-flight footballer changing hands for a cumulative total of £6 million during his peak years. The midfielder was also an England international during his time at Hillsborough although he tasted relegation with Wednesday in 1989/90 – his first full season with the Owls. That feeling was nothing new. He had been demoted with West Bromwich Albion four years earlier and though the Baggies escaped a further drop down the ranks just two seasons later – surviving by a single point as Sheffield United took the fall – he managed to stave off such disappointments for almost a decade during stints at Leeds United and Southampton. Nottingham Forest, or rather former Wednesday boss Ron Atkinson, invested a six-figure sum to acquire his services in January 1999. The transfer was arranged within a week of the new manager coming in as Forest battled to beat the Premier League drop. But the gamble failed. That prompted a move to Coventry City and though Palmer was loaned to Watford and Sheffield Wednesday for much of the 2000/01 season he bore some culpability for the Sky Blues having their tenure in the elite ranks ended. As Stockport County's player/manager Carlton chalked up a fifth relegation – this time from Division One – after being drafted in as a long-term replacement for Andy Kilner. An ailing season could not be reversed and though he kept the Hatters stable in the third tier an inability to make progress led to his dismissal. There has only been one promotion during Palmer's career as the Owls left Division Two in 1991.

SOWING THE SEED OF DISCONTENT

When Wednesday staved off the threat of relegation in 1928 they did so at the expense of Tottenham Hotspur and with the aid of Jimmy Seed who, in an ironic twist, was allowed a Hillsborough transfer as Spurs thought the 32-year-old had nothing to offer them. Prior to using the inside-forward as bait to lure Arthur 'Darkie' Lowdell to North London, they had cut Seed's wages by £1 per week and denied him an opportunity to join Guildford United as player/manager. The County Durham man showed no signs that he harboured any resentment. If only they had a crystal ball at White Hart Lane, Seed may have proved an integral part of a fight against the drop offering not just his footballing skills but experience and the motivational abilities teams needed to galvanise a survival bid. Those assets were certainly utilised at Hillsborough. Seed was named skipper and despite some tribulations over the 1927/28 season's first half dozen months, his appointment proved a wise one. Wednesday were bottom of Division One with ten games remaining and trailing safety by 7 points after a disappointing 4–2 defeat at Bury. 17 points from the 20 available (which included a double over Spurs in the space of just four days, Seed scoring in both) allowed the Owls to reach safety while the once well placed Tottenham fell like a stone.

Twelve months later Wednesday benefited from the other side of Seed's game. As team fortunes changed so did his captaincy. Now he inspired his troops to the glory of a league title – a task he proved himself more than capable of discharging. Before leaving the club in 1931 due to a knee injury which had limited his effectiveness for a few seasons he led the Owls to another championship. After retiring he made a successful stab at club management steering Charlton Athletic to the FA Cup in 1947. But for agreeing to take the helm at Charlton in September 1933, Seed may have managed Wednesday who sought his services when Bob Brown left the hot-seat.

DEADLINE DAY

The sale of Bob Whittingham and English McConnell to Chelsea in April 1910 effectively led to the introduction of a transfer window. The Londoners were hoping to avoid relegation to Division Three and though their bid was unsuccessful, calls to limit clubs with better finances from buying their way out of trouble while less prosperous clubs struggled increased. A year after the pair made that switch a date in March was set by which all activity had to be completed.

ON BORROWED TIME

In late October 1974 Wednesday signed Eric McCordie on loan from Middlesbrough and found this early experience of borrowing another club's player fruitful. The Northern Ireland international came down a division and before leaving eight weeks later had scored 6 goals in 9 league games. That contribution wasn't enough to stop Wednesday falling into Division Three but it made McMordie the club's top scorer that term. There was a hope of retaining the player but a full transfer could not be agreed. How the season may otherwise have panned out is unknown but there remains a chance that a drop may have been avoided.

Warren Feeney who joined the Owls from Cardiff City in late November 2009 on a month's loan has one of the shortest Wednesday careers, lasting just 13 minutes. Brian Laws drafted him in but left the manager's post eight days after that substitute debut in a 2–0 home defeat by Reading – a last win had been 7 games and almost two months earlier. Over the weeks which remained of his stay, Feeney failed to figure in first-team plans.

MASCOT MANIA

A well-known feature of the modern game is the club mascot. Unsurprisingly, Wednesday chose an Owl but the club had employed the custom well ahead of others. Complete with a straw-boater hat, Ozzie debuted in January 1967 in the fashion of a cartoon drawing. He retired for almost two decades before returning in the Premiership era – this time in person rather than just as a sketch. He was joined by nephews Ollie from late 1994 and more recently Bazz. All three could be seen parading up and down the pitch at Hillsborough until 2006 when replaced by Barney Owl who had a far softer look and image than his predecessors. Ozzie Owl made a comeback in January 2009 and was joined by a new Barney.

A MONKEY ON HIS BACK

For a short period of time – just one game – a monkey dressed in blue and white was employed as one of football's earliest mascots. The primate, given the name Jacko, was donated by a Wednesday fan who found himself located in Southampton and brought the animal back from a visit across the high seas to India. Jacko was passed on to James McConnell and led the team out for a cup tie with Glossop North End. A 1–0 defeat made many question just how much luck had been brought. Jacko failed to reappear while McConnell was referred to as Monkey throughout his career.

SHEFFIELD LIFE NO BLAST FOR ERIC

After receiving a two-month ban for an indiscretion which started with hurling a ball at a referee and ended by calling an entire disciplinary committee idiots, Eric Cantona announced his retirement. Backtracking on that initial decision the 25-year-old consulted two men to act as advisors – France manager Michel Platini and his assistant, Gérard Houllier. Wednesday were interested but then manager Trevor Francis had practical difficulties. Cantona's club, Nîmes, needed pre-agreed compensation of £1 million. Paying such a large sum for someone with a long history of disorder, no matter how gifted, carried risk though it seemed a loan deal was possible after trials. On Cantona's side there was an apparent understanding that only a medical needed to be passed. However, having already travelled to South Yorkshire when these differences came to light, Cantona decided to see the week-long audition through. Harsh weather made a conventional training session impossible so work moved to an indoor complex where some basic fitness was done and five-a-sides played.

A hat-trick and some impressive contributions in a full-scale match on artificial surfacing boded well and there was an opportunity to see more in the shape of an indoor six-a-side match with Baltimore Blast at the Sheffield Arena. The Frenchman was clearly keen to impress and gave the game as much as he could but when not playing appeared forlorn. A continued impossibility to work outdoors troubled Francis who was unwilling to take a risk without at least a full viewing on grass. He suggested another week's stay but Cantona had little interest in extending the trial and no accommodation could be reached. In total he spent four days with Wednesday and having swallowed some pride already felt anything more would be too humbling. Soon after the French international was being paraded around Elland Road and when the season ended so was the Football League championship trophy. Wednesday were 7 points behind Leeds United in third place, wondering just what might have been if a gamble had been taken.

A PAGE IN HISTORY

A successful auction bid via the Wednesday website saw Andrew Page from Lancaster beat off competition to land a place in the Owls' 2002/03 squad. Though not expected to play, that possibility nonetheless remained for the 25-year-old auxiliary nurse who involved himself in a range of activities around the club.

MINOR HONOURS

Wednesday won the first Sheffield Challenge Cup competition in sensational fashion with a 4–3 win over Heeley FC in 1877 and throughout the next 10 years lifted the trophy five times. Bending the rules both teams fielded 12 players in their starting line-up. The trophy itself was designed by students of the Sheffield College of Art and crafted by Martin Hall Co. who manufactured the original FA Cup. Now known as the Sheffield and Hallamshire Senior Cup, it has been lifted 14 times by sides representing Wednesday and the club remains the most successful in the competition's history despite not registering a win since 1954 when the 'A' team beat Worksop Town. Wednesday withdrew from the competition not long after. Added to that 'A' team honour are 6 first-team wins and 7 from the reserves.

CUPS, BOWLS & SHIELDS

In 1879 Wednesday became the first winners of the Wharncliffe Charity Cup beating old foes Heeley in the final. A growing superiority in the city was underlined by capturing the cup five more times over the subsequent nine years. Heeley were the opposition three years later when another 5 goals were scored – this time all in Wednesday's favour. The trophy was retained 12 months later courtesy of a 4–0 win over Pye Bank. In 1886 Heeley made it a hat-trick of defeats when they were on the receiving end of a 2–0 scoreline – the same margin of defeat suffered by Rotherham in 1888. Despite seeming to be fall guys Heeley did beat Wednesday in the 1880 and 1885 finals. As did Staveley who effectively denied the club a hat-trick in 1887 when victory would have formed the middle part of three successive wins from 1886 to 1888. Although consigned to history a long time ago, the Wharncliffe Cup did survive into the twentieth century and was won by Wednesday's second string in 1903.

Wednesday became the first winners of a specially arranged tournament called the Plymouth Bowl aimed at promoting the professional game in the coastal town. Notts County were beaten 2–0 at Home Park by goals from Jock Malloch and Harry Ruddlesdin. The Sheriff of London's Charity Shield – won 2–0 against Corinthians at Crystal Palace in 1905 – added one more item of silverware to a burgeoning trophy cabinet during the early part of the last century. Andrew Wilson grabbed both goals.

WALKER DOWN UNDER

In his brief stay at Hillsborough, Colin Walker, Rotherham born and bred, spent more time playing for New Zealand than Wednesday. He made three senior outings, scoring a hat-trick in just 12 minutes during his bow – a 7–0 pummelling of Stockport County in the League Cup after coming off the bench. A treble against Fiji – a side he scored against on international debut – helped the forward grab 18 goals from 34 All White caps. International recognition was gained after attaining New Zealand citizenship during his lengthy stint with Gisborne City. The forward's links with Wednesday stretch right back to his boyhood. As an 11-year-old he was the Owls' mascot for the last game of the 1969/70 season – a 2–1 defeat by eventual FA Cup winners Manchester City. Wednesday needed a win to avoid going down.

ROYAL APPOINTMENTS

Although far from a regular at Hillsborough, the current monarch, Queen Elizabeth II, has paid official visits to S6. The first was during a trip to Sheffield almost 18 months after her coronation – one of her first domestic duties after a half-year tour of the Commonwealth. Her trip took in the ground where a large crowd assembled. Thirty-two years later Her Majesty returned to commemorate the addition of a roof on the Spion Kop in December 1986.

SCANDAL

In December 1962 Ipswich Town entertained Sheffield Wednesday in a First Division game. There were few spectacular instances and no obvious signs of players creating incidents, which led to defeat. The East Anglians were regular victors when the pair met and the match seemed to have been lost fairly and squarely. However, a little over a year later *Sunday People* journalists claimed they had evidence of match-fixing and said three Wednesday players had placed bets on their own team losing this match. In January 1965 charges of match-fixing or conspiracy to fix matches were proven against 10 of those involved from the Nottingham area. The player identified as the ring leader, Jimmy Gauld, received a four-year prison sentence and liability for £5,000 costs. It was learned that a fee of £7,420 was handed over by the newspaper in exchange for Gauld's story. The Aberdonian had seen his career ended by a broken leg at the turn of the 1960s and since became heavily involved in fixing results. He had winnings from bookmakers estimated at £3,275.

Three other players, David Layne, Tony Kay (who was signed by Everton just weeks after the match in question took place) and Peter Swan, each received four-month prison sentences. Layne, who was heard in taped conversations with Gauld, tried to take all the blame and pleaded guilty. Only Swan, who denied any involvement in this coup, entered the witness box where he admitted betting on other games he knew to be rigged. The incident robbed Swan of his chance to play in and win the 1966 World Cup. Alf Ramsey had told him that a place in the centre of defence was his but after the scandal future Wednesday boss Jack Charlton took it.

None of those involved were allowed to attend games. For Swan, who lived so close to Hillsborough that he could hear the crowd and had a son looking to make the professional grade, that was a huge blow. Even playing pub football was barred and one team received a heavy fine for allowing Swan to turn out. Those life bans were reversed after eight years but only Swan managed a comeback with Wednesday. However, at 36 years old his impact was so limited he rejected an offer to remain at Hillsborough and joined Bury, who he scored for after 3 minutes of his debut having never netted for Wednesday. Layne returned but failed to progress beyond the reserves and after a loan spell with Hereford United left professional football. Kay never looked at anything beyond amateur status. Uncorroborated statements from the player state that he was asked to explain the finer points of taped evidence to the Kray twins ahead of one of their trials.

BIG VICTORIES

Wednesday's largest victory came in the opening round of the 1890/91 FA Cup. Halliwell were easily beaten 12–0 on 17 January at Hillsborough. Toddles Woolhouse scored 5 of the dozen. In the Football League a 9–1 hammering of Birmingham City on 13 December 1930 still stands as the record although had the Owls managed to build on the 7 goals they hit before half time against Sunderland on Boxing Day 1911, that mark could well have been bettered. However, Wednesday only managed one more strike over the second period. The win over Birmingham capped a 7-match streak in which the club hit a massive 36 goals.

BESTS ...

Fewest goals conceded	22	Div 2	1899/1900 (also constitutes a record for Division 2)
Fewest defeats	5	Div 2	1899/1900 (34 game season)
	6	Div 2	1983/84 (42 game season)
Most goals scored	106	Div 2	1958/59
Most points	62	Div 2	1958/59 (2 points for a win)
	88	Div 2	1983/84 (3 points for a win)
Most wins	28	Div 2	1958/59

... AND WORSTS

Most goals conceded	100	Div 1	1954/55
Most defeats	26	Div 1	1919/20
	26	Div 2	1974/75
Fewest goals scored	28	Div 1	1919/20
Fewest points	21	Div 2	1974/75 (2 points for a win)
	31	Prem	1999/2000 (3 points for a win)
Fewest wins		Div 2	1974/75

DOUBLE NO TROUBLE

Beating teams twice over a single season – a double – is a tricky feat. Many teams struggle to register more than half a dozen per term. Wednesday's best is eight in a single season which has been achieved on five occasions: 1899/1900, 1925/26, 1929/30, 1958/59 and 1983/84.

BROTHER, CAN YOU SPARE A DIME?

In the Football Alliance's last season before its merger with the rival Football League, Wednesday needed to dip a hand in their own pockets to ensure a fixture with Birmingham St George was fulfilled. Money was a scarce commodity for most sides but especially for the stricken Saints whose secretary had alerted his Owlerton counterpart that club funds were all but exhausted. Title-chasing Wednesday needed points and used financial gains from hosting Bolton Wanderers in the FA Cup plus some lucrative friendlies with clubs north of the border to fund their opponents' trip up from the Midlands. St George returned home nursing their pride after a 4–0 hammering and were forced to fold when the season ended. One of their players, Harry Davis, impressed and was signed by Wednesday.

WAR GAMES

Despite the First World War starting in 1914, it took the best part of two years for the Football League to suspend activities. Teams kept playing but in specially arranged contests and from September 1915 to April 1919 Wednesday took part in the Midland Section (Principal Tournament). The Midland Section (Subsidiary Tournament) was introduced for the last half-dozen games of a campaign.

The advent of the Second World War was a totally different matter. The possible repercussions of an all-out conflict were plain for all to see and it meant the 1939/40 league campaign was just 3 games old when abandoned. War became inevitable hours before Wednesday took on Plymouth Argyle at Hillsborough on Wednesday 2 September 1939 as Germany refused to pull troops out of occupied Poland. Regional divisions were set up once more but unlike those established during the previous hostilities, these allowed many changes to both the game rules and personnel to ensure Ministry of Defence guidelines on travel, crowding and air raids were satisfied. Wednesday saw 50 men go to war over six years of conflict. The Owls originally joined the East Midlands Regional Division but subsequently opted for the North Regional Division who decided their league placings purely on the basis of goals scored and conceded.

A modicum of success was achieved in reaching the League North War Cup Final in 1943, although Blackpool won the two-legged encounter. When the teams drew 2–2 at Bloomfield Road it seemed Wednesday were in the driving seat but a 2–1 home defeat sealed victory for the Seasiders. Jackie Robinson scored in both games. A number of impressive performances in the league – especially for Robinson who scored 6 hat-tricks – saw Wednesday land third place.

Guesting, a system which allowed professionals to turn out for teams close to their military postings, was introduced. Charlie Tomlinson made a return despite being transferred to Bradford Park Avenue just before war was declared. He had been allowed to leave due to doubts about his ability to make the necessary standard but did so much to prove his former employers wrong that Wednesday re-signed him for £1,000. One player who enjoyed great success with the club during this period was Frank Melling who scored 35 goals in 55 games after making his debut in September 1941. This form was widely expected to earn him a playing contract once football got back to normal but Melling decided to take up the option of a university place. He rebuffed all Wednesday's approaches, eventually becoming a long-standing member of Sheffield United's board.

Established Wednesday players such as Redfern Froggatt continued to play for the Owls – duties permitting. Tom Cawley saw out the First World War with Wednesday but made a brief defection to Bradford when City turned up at Hillsborough one man short. A quick-fire loan deal was made but Wednesday's generosity backfired when Cawley grabbed a brace in the 3–1 defeat.

OLYMPIC OWLS

Dave Russell failed to return to Sheffield Wednesday after the war. In fact he decided not to come back to Britain after being demobbed from the RAF, accepting an offer to coach Danish outfit Odense. Matters went well and two years on he was working with Denmark's national team – led by Englishman Reg Mountford – guiding the Scandanavians to an Olympic bronze in 1948 with a win over hosts Great Britain. Eighteen months later he took the reins at Bury then became a stalwart at Tranmere Rovers where he served for over two decades.

Keeper Hadyn Henry Clifford Hill made four outings for Wednesday – the last eight months before representing Great Britain at the 1936 Berlin Olympics. His games for the Owls tended to be high-scoring affairs and his appearances in Germany were little different. He did keep a clean sheet against China but conceded 5 when Poland won by the odd goal in 9.

THREE TIMES A CHARM

Former Wednesday midfielder John Sheridan has sought to prove his managerial credentials in the lower leagues and despite some disappointment with Oldham Athletic, helped Chesterfield gain promotion to League One. The Spireites were confirmed as divisional champions on the last day of the 2010/11 season meaning the former Republic of Ireland international is the third ex-Owl to steward the club to a promotion. Teddy Davison (1930/31) and William Harvey (1935/36) both guided their sides to Third Division North titles.

TO THE FOUR

The 1992/93 season was a unique term for the club who became the first to make four appearances at Wembley in a single campaign. The Owls appeared in the League and FA Cup finals which were both lost to Arsenal. The other two Wembley days came in the replayed FA Cup semi-final with Sheffield United held at the national stadium due to an unprecedented demand for tickets.

LOOK INTO MY EYES

A career path once seemed mapped out for ex-professionals as on hanging up their boots they could enter coaching or otherwise remain involved in the game. There was also the option of becoming a publican. However, some former Owls have plied a number of very different trades. Perhaps one of the most intriguing professions pursued is that undertaken by Pat Heard. On his retirement he took a number of jobs but eventually became known as stage hypnotist Patrick Stewart. Klas Ingesson became a lumberjack in his native Sweden.

I PROPOSE

Wednesday keeper Robert Burch risked a little leg-pulling in the dressing room by proposing to his girlfriend of six years on live television. Having discussed the plan with goalkeeping coach, fellow stopper Lee Grant and most importantly his mum, he arranged the gesture. His intended, a producer on ITV's *This Morning* show, received a large bunch of red roses and an offer of marriage during a broadcast on Valentine's Day 2008. With Fern Britton in close attendance the answer was yes and the pair tied the knot a year later.

EYE BLINK

Regi Blinker has been something of a success on and off the pitch. In addition to running a number of businesses the former Dutch international has also undertaken plenty of charitable work. This includes running marathons and becoming the first person to abseil down Harrods department store. During his days at Hillsborough a little personal gain led to some hilarity. A large sponsorship deal was offered by a brand of designer sunglasses. However, the company had believed they were recruiting Edgar Davids to their cause who wore darkened glasses for an eye condition. Both were born in Suriname, represented the Netherlands and sported dreadlocks, but the corporate executive clearly didn't know his football.

FASTER THAN A CANNONBALL

Journalists often describe shots with clichés such as howitzers, cannonballs or even thunderbolts. All subjective terms which convey the power packed into an effort but technological advances have made the measuring of the hardest shot in domestic football possible. The current holder is David Hirst, who thumped the ball past David Seaman from 14.8 yards at a speed of 114mph in September 1996. Unfortunately it thudded against the crossbar and bounced to safety. Wednesday were one up at Highbury but eventually lost 4–1.

No other shot in an English competition has so far passed three figures. The closest is a David Beckham's strike at 97.7mph. Richie Humphreys' screamer for the Owls against Aston Villa a month before Hirst's rocket had Michael Oakes thankful not to have got a hand on the left-footed volley, as it whistled by at a virtually pedestrian 95.9mph. Crucially, it hit the net. The boyhood Blade made that contribution in just his sixth senior outing.

REALITY BITES BUT NOT MAN'S BEST FRIEND

Gilles de Bilde has been a serial competitor on Belgian TV reality shows. Along with his third-place finish in a version of *Strictly Come Dancing*, he appeared on *Celebrity Shock* and a show entitled *Homeless World Cup* in which he coached his nation's homeless football squad. The striker was far from a popular figure at Hillsborough and turned down a loan move to Aston Villa as he could find no one to look after his dogs. It was once alleged that the hounds which scuppered his move to the Midlands – two Dobermans – were smuggled into the UK contravening quarantine laws. His penchant for pooches saw him miss a game with Belgian third tier outfit Willebroek Meerhof towards the end of his career in September 2006 when one of his pets died.

Another former Owl to appear in reality or celebrity-based shows is Bruce Grobbelaar who worked under Marco Pierre White's stewardship in *Hell's Kitchen*.

TYNAN'S GOT TALENT

Not long before his 16th birthday, young Liverpudlian Thomas Tynan, a striker who had represented the city's schools, entered a *Liverpool Echo* backed competition to find a star footballer of tomorrow. He had only shown enough promise to make the county's junior grades failing to be selected for the upper age ranges. He played for a modest local club so was possibly not expecting much to come from the opportunity, but after collecting tokens printed in the paper he got a trial and was quickly into the last 100 boys. When the number was pared down to a mere 20 he was in the final shake up and invited to participate in some five-a-sides.

Two games were played and he grabbed 5 goals in each. Liverpool Football Club had dispatched their head of youth development to the event and while he didn't approach Tynan on the night, he obtained the youngster's details and invited him for training. He jumped at the chance and was given terms after maintaining his impressive form then helping the club reach the 1972 FA Youth Cup final. Within the year he had progressed even further and joined the reserves. However, that was as far as his Anfield career developed and in 1976, without a first-team outing, Tynan joined Sheffield Wednesday playing over 100 games across all competitions in just over two seasons. It was at Newport County and Plymouth Argyle that the forward played most of his near 700 Football League appearances. He also served Lincoln City, Rotherham United, Torquay United and Doncaster Rovers chalking up more than 300 goals during his lengthy career.

TIGHT FIT

Italians are noted for their sartorial elegance – largely. One of Wednesday's most notorious imports from that country, Paolo Di Canio, had a penchant which veered away from the 1990s preference for baggy shorts. In a retro touch reminiscent of many kits from the previous decade Paolo insisted on wearing tighter-fitting and smaller shorts than any of his team-mates. It was a stance he maintained throughout most of his career. On one occasion – while at West Ham United he wore them backwards. The fashion faux pas was unintentional but he kept them that way for luck.

PLENTY IN RESERVE

Wednesday's second string have fared well since gaining the chance to enjoy league football each week of the season. The club only had a league to partake in from 1891 when the Sheffield and Hallamshire League was formed. After a sole season the reserves moved on to the Sheffield and District League. These parochial engagements were placed to one side just ahead of the twentieth century by gaining a place in the Midland League where many of the top clubs had representatives. Additionally some of the best clubs outside the Football League plied their trades within its structures. Consequently, lifting the title in 1903 was no mean feat. The crown was Wednesday's again in two of the next five seasons which underpinned the quality on hand. Just one more top-place finish was secured – in 1923, the last season before the Owls joined the Central League.

This next step was also a hefty stride up the reserve structure. Almost exclusively populated by the strongest professional sides, as a result of members defecting to the Football League's recently created third tier, the going was much tougher but those on the fringe of the Wednesday first team drew immense benefit, and honours when the 1928/29 season saw the club finish in pole position. That win was only followed by another just after the war. Thirty years separated the next two triumphs – in 1960/61 and 1990/91. After a stint in the Premier League's own competition there was a return in the early 2000s. By this time regional organisations had been introduced which saw the Owls placed in the Central Division which they won in 2005/06. Two campaigns earlier Wednesday lifted the Central League Cup for the first and only time. In 2011 the club stepped away from the practice of having much organised football between the senior and youth teams. A decision to arrange games with small bends to the rules if appropriate was plumped for. Rolling substitutions and irregular game times among other things would serve the club better, according to Gary Megson.

LEAGUE RECORD

Football League Record

1892	Elected to the Football League Division One
1899–1900	Division Two
1900–20	Division One
1920–6	Division Two
1926–37	Division One
1937–50	Division Two
1950–1	Division One
1951–2	Division Two
1952–5	Division One
1955–6	Division Two
1956–8	Division One
1958–9	Division Two
1959–70	Division One
1970–5	Division Two
1980–4	Division Two
1984–90	Division One
1990–1	Division Two
1991–2	Division One
1992–2000	Premier League
2000–3	Division One
2003–4	Division Two
2004–5	League One
2005–10	Championship
2010–	League One

ONE & ONLY

To date only a couple of players have scored in their first and only appearance for Wednesday. G.A. Johnson was the first and may have expected at least one more chance after completing the 4–0 thumping of Blackpool on 4 April 1931. The other member of this exclusive list is Jack Lindsay who pulled one back in a 4–2 defeat by Barnsley on 2 September 1946.

INJURY TIME

Although some players manage to carry on with their careers after debilitating injuries, Scott Oakes, who joined the Owls in a high-profile £425,000 deal ahead of the 1996/97 season, was frustrated by a host of niggling setbacks. David Pleat who had previously managed the midfielder at both Leicester City and Luton Town – and bought a player specifically to trade with the Foxes in order to land Oakes – was unable to call on the man he coveted so much. With Luton having been freshly relegated to the third tier and Wednesday a Premier League club there was a huge gulf for Scott to bridge, but he made some notable contributions at times and often looked comfortable among the elite. The second season was a harder slog and when called upon it was usually as a substitute. Only one outing came from the bench in the season which followed – a despairing 4–0 defeat at Middlesbrough. Over the 1999/2000 campaign – his last with the Owls – Scott found himself wholly outside the first team picture. In four seasons he made 27 senior appearances, only seven of which were from the beginning of a game.

TAKE A SEAT ON THE BENCH

In an era where the number of substitutes able to be named, and the amount of changes a manager could make was also more limited, Trevor Francis made 51 runs outs from the bench – 47 of these were league appearances between 1990 and 1993 (many under his own management).

Other players to have spent a large amount of time on the bench are Gordon Watson who, despite making 47 starts, was brought on 44 times, while Mark Chamberlain was called into the action more times than he started games. He made 38 full appearances but appeared as a substitute on 47 occasions; 34 of these were in the Football League and 18 in the 1985/86 season. Of the 66 times Nigel Jemson pulled on a Wednesday shirt, 33 were from the opening whistle and 33 while he wore the number 12 or 14 shirt.

The most substitutes used by the club in a single season prior to the rule which allowed up to three in a single game are the 36 Len Ashurst employed during the 1975/76 campaign.

BEST OF TIMES

On 9 August 2005, just five days into his loan from fellow Championship side Southampton, and on the day he scored the first goal of his senior career, Leon Best broke a bone in his foot and returned to St Mary's. Recovering within four months he was allowed back to Hillsborough the following January and scored again in the last of his 11 additional appearances.

FIRST IMPRESSIONS

Outstanding debuts are usually measured in terms of exceptional performances or goals scored. However, some first outings are memorable for totally different reasons. Colin Dobson for example played his first game in a Wednesday shirt a full five years after signing for the club in September 1961. He used the time to finish his apprenticeship on the shipyards ensuring he had a future outside the game.

NAMESAKES

Two Wednesday players have shared the name Harry Davis. The original is said by some to have scored Wednesday's first league goal in the game with Notts County but whatever the truth of that claim there is very little doubt about the others he scored until his departure four years later. He left the club in 1896 after appearing in Wednesday's first ever cup win.

A second Harry Davis joined the Owls at the turn of the century helping Wednesday to promotion and making a 13-goal contribution to the title win of 1902/03. Although fairly small in stature he did make up for his lack of inches in many other ways. After making himself an essential member of the Owls side he was unfortunate to miss out on the 1907 FA Cup win. A broken leg suffered in the third round replay with Sunderland ruled him out and effectively ended his playing career. Once officially retired he joined Wednesday's coaching staff.

A couple of David Johnsons have also been on the Hillsborough books. The Dinnington-born forward of that name emerged through the youth ranks but failed to find the net in the handful of opportunities offered during the 1990s before a transfer to Lincoln City. David Johnson the Jamaican international had changed hands for fees totalling more than £5 million by his mid-twenties but Nottingham Forest allowed a loan to Wednesday during the spring of 2002. He was experiencing something of a goal drought as his first full term drew to its close. Two in seven outings with the Owls helped boost confidence and a far better second season was enjoyed at the City Ground.

Although referred to as James Quinn and Jimmy Quinn respectively, ultimately this pair share the same forename. The latter, who converted from centre forward to left-back, had a brief stay at Hillsborough after coming down from Celtic in 1974. Coventry-born Northern Ireland international James signed a short-term deal in 2005 after being released by Dutch side Willem II.

QUESTION TIME

Television has tried to marry football with quiz shows on many occasions and met with varying degrees of success. One of the earliest was BBC1's *Quizball* screened during the late 1960s and early 1970s. Football teams were represented by three players or officials plus a celebrity supporter. Answering questions correctly allowed a 'goal' to be scored.

Wednesday were enthusiastic participants during the early years debuting in 1966 for the first series, although they were ultimately edged out by Dunfermline Athletic. Owls coach David Smith joined players Sam Ellis and Wilf Smith plus celebrity supporter Leonard Sachs. The actor had well-established links with another Yorkshire city and represented Leeds United three years later – Wednesday were not participating.

Author Stan Barstow was on duty 12 months later coming in alongside David Ford, Gerry Young and assistant boss John Marshall. Barstow found his way onto the scoresheet though once again Scottish opposition, in the shape of Hearts, proved too strong.

WELCOME TO THE BIG TIME

Though attached to Wednesday on an amateur basis Trevor Pearson was turning out in local leagues on the weekend for a couple of clubs. Weekdays saw him earn a crust as an apprentice engineer. Even his involvement in the Owls reserves was minimal. However, in March 1972 with two keepers – Peter Springett and Peter Grummitt – injured, Derek Dooley had no option but to dig deep inside his squad. It left a couple of teenagers; 16-year-old Kevin Wilson and the ever so slightly more mature 19-year-old Pearson. What tipped the scales is unknown but most likely it was those extra few months' experience and more regular games. Despite conceding four on his debut at Fulham, there was a pick-up of results if not necessarily outcomes in the three other games he featured in.

HE WORE LONG KNICKERS

In January 1920 temperatures across the country dropped. Snow tumbled down, too. As a winger, Southampton-born Bill Harvey would feel the cold. Stuck out on the flanks there was little warmth on offer unless you had the ball – not even close proximity to the crowd helped. To keep himself as warm as possible in an FA Cup replay with Darlington, Harvey plumped to play in the knickerbocker-style shorts popular in the game's early days – also ones with pockets for his hands. The non-league outfit pulled off a shock beating their First Division opponents – albeit struggling ones – 2–0 at Hillsborough.

AWAY ALL THE WAY

In the FA Cup between January 1962 and the same month in 1967, Wednesday failed to gain a single home draw, but still reached Wembley in 1966. Leaving replays and the neutral venues from that unprecedented run to the final aside – from welcoming Nottingham Forest to Hillsborough until a pairing with Queens Park Rangers in the above months where there was a possibility of gaining a home draw – ten successive rounds went by without the welcome mat being rolled out in the Owlerton district

OLD IRON

Joe Cockroft, a player who went on to figure hugely in Wednesday's modern history, spent much of the early seasons of the Second World War with pre-conflict employers West Ham United. He won the 1940 League War Cup in their colours. A requirement to work at Edgar Allen's Steelworks saw him come to Sheffield. During 203 war games he helped the Owls reach the League North Cup final. However, despite his first-leg penalty Wednesday went on to lose the tie on aggregate scores. An official debut for the elegant wing-half came just months before his 35th birthday, in the FA Cup. After falling just short of a century of appearances he joined Sheffield United where he became the Football League's oldest debutant.

MATCH ABANDONED

From frost to waterlogged pitches, the elements have at times frustrated the Owls' efforts to finish a game. So too have officials and some less than gentlemanly conduct. On 6 April 1895, in a match with Stoke, the referee, Mr Lewis, irked a crowd which readily recalled some decisions they had been dissatisfied with against Sunderland two weeks earlier. With 15 minutes remaining the official cracked when a piece of grass was thrown at him by a fan and he called an early halt to proceedings. The encounter was goalless but 11 days on when the match was restaged the Potters won 4–2 with the points aiding their relegation fight.

OTHER SPORTS AT HILLSBOROUGH

Other sports to have been staged at Hillsborough include boxing and tennis – some exhibition matches took place during the summer of 1939. The Harlem Globetrotters basketball team were regular visitors to Yorkshire and in 1957 their tour of England took in the stadium. During the 1989/90 Rugby League season Sheffield Eagles entertained St Helens and Wigan at Wednesday's home after safety concerns meant their Owlerton Stadium base could not be used for the sport.

DERRING DON'T

Daredevil rider Evel Knievel would have performed at Hillsborough in 1975 had he not been forced to cancel as a result of one his most notorious failures to complete a stunt. The American's show at Wembley Stadium on 25 May was broadcast across the world and an estimated 90,000 people were present to see an attempt to jump 13 single-decker buses. A broken hand, pelvis and vertebra – three of 433 breaks or fractures he suffered – resulted from the crash. It also saw him announce his retirement there and then. Via the PA he said 'Ladies and gentlemen of this wonderful country, I have to tell you that you are the last people in the world who will see me jump. Because I will never, ever, ever jump again. I'm through.' That said, Five months later Knievel was back performing.

PLAYING BY NUMBERS

Players are now intrinsically linked to a squad number, but prior to 1928 shirts contained no distinguishing marks. On 25 August that year, Wednesday helped trial a system where positions on the pitch were assigned a specific digit from 1 to 11. Arsenal were the visitors to Hillsborough for the experiment. Elsewhere on the day only a match featuring Chelsea and Swansea Town took place under the same conditions. Of more concern to most inside the stadium was that the Owls won by the odd goal in five.

It took more than a decade for the Football League to introduce the system on a permanent basis. In July 1939 its management committee, which had also used a system where one team would wear numbers 1 to 11 while the other would sport 12 to 22, opted to adopt one where both sides wore the same numbers.

BENDING THE RULES

Never shy of causing a little controversy, Gary Megson set about finding a way around the Johnstone's Paint Trophy rules by making all three of his permitted substitutions within the opening 18 minutes of an opening round match with Bradford City in August 2011. Competition regulations state that at least six regular first team members should start a game. Megson duly obliged but withdrew keeper Nicky Weaver on two minutes then made a double swap just over a quarter of an hour later ending the participation of David Prutton and Jose Semedo. The Owls lost 3–1 on penalties.